Shorties

SELT — STUDIES IN ENGLISH LANGUAGE TEACHING

Augsburger Studien zur Englischdidaktik

Edited by Engelbert Thaler (Augsburg)

Volume 1

Engelbert Thaler (ed.)

Shorties

Flash Fiction in English Language Teaching

Bibliografische Information der Deutschen Nationalbibliothek

Die Deutsche Nationalbibliothek verzeichnet diese Publikation in der Deutschen Nationalbib-
liografie; detaillierte bibliografische Daten sind im Internet über http://dnb.dnb.de abrufbar.

© 2016 · Narr Francke Attempto Verlag GmbH + Co. KG
Dischingerweg 5 · D-72070 Tübingen

Internet: www.narr.de
E-Mail: info@narr.de

Printed in Germany

ISSN 2367-3826
ISBN 978-3-8233-6997-4

Contents

Introduction

»Brevity is the soul of wit« – Polonius' famous dictum in William Shakespeare's *Hamlet* (2, ii) also applies to SHORTIES. Short narrative texts are valuable material for the language classroom because they are short and narrative – and often witty.

In contrast to Polonius' follow-up statement to King Claudius and Hamlet's mother Gertrude »I will be brief. Your noble son is mad«, shorties are anything but »mad«. They are flexible in use, can comfortably be dealt with in a single lesson, appear in a multitude of forms, can bridge the gap between coursebooks and »Literature with a capital 'L'«, are increasing their popularity in the digital era, can promote all language competences, fulfil anthropological and psychological needs, and are an omnipresent phenomenon in everyday life. Man's desire to tell or listen to stories has even caused the American philosopher Walter Fisher to relabel man: from *homo sapiens* to *homo narrans*.

But where is *homo narrans* – or the *storytelling animal* (Alasdair MacIntyre) – in the classroom? Given this multivalency, it is astonishing that shorties have been neglected in foreign language teaching. The traditional *short story* has always been an integral part of language learning. Yet the *short short stories* may have been regarded too short to be accepted as aesthetically dignified literature worth being treated in the classroom.

It seems high time to plead for the inclusion of *flash fiction* in TEFL (Teaching English as a Foreign Language). This style of fictional literature of extreme brevity appears in a huge number of varieties – from realist, surreal, hyperrealist forms to psychological, impressionist, essayistic types up to satirical, social-critical, or parabolic texts. As there is no widely accepted definition of the length of this genre, any narrative text between 6 and 1,000 words may be subsumed among the categories of flash fiction or shorties. Dramatic and lyrical texts can, of course, also be very short, but will not be treated as shorties here.

This book, as all edited volumes in the SELT (Studies in English Language Teaching) series, follows a **triple aim**:
1. Linking TEFL with related academic disciplines
2. Balancing TEFL research and classroom practice
3. Combining theory, methodology and exemplary lessons

This triple aim is reflected in the **three-part structure** of this volume. In Part A (Theory), the topic of shorties and flash fiction is investigated from the perspectives of three academic disciplines, i.e. from the viewpoints of TEFL, literary studies and linguistics. Part B (Methodology) assembles six contributions on selected texts, media and techniques. Nine concrete lesson plans can be found in Part C (Classroom). These lessons were designed by lecturer and students at university, then conducted and assessed by 13 teachers at German schools, and finally revised by the editor. Each of these nine chapters is divided into genre (brief background information on the text type), procedure (source, synopsis, competences, topics, level, time, phases of the lesson), materials (texts, worksheets, board sketches), solutions (expected answers), and bibliography.

Part A is introduced by the TEFL perspective. **Engelbert Thaler** gives a few answers to the six W and one H questions: What? (Definition) Why? (Rationale) When? (Level) Where? (Venues) Which? (Types) What for? (Objectives) How? (Methods). With regard to the basic issues of selection, methodology and objectives, he draws a triple conclusion: After the short story has long been accepted as a popular genre in TEFL, it is high time to use shorter short stories and flash fiction as well. Teachers should strike a fair balance between analytical and creative procedures. With the help of shorties, narrative competence concerning receptive and productive skills should be promoted.

The perspective of **literary studies** is adopted by **Timo Müller**. He focuses on the formal features and the didactic potential of the short short story in general. After a brief historical overview, he situates the short short story in relation to other genres, discusses the reading strategies it demands, and illustrates his findings by the example of Joseph Bruchac's story »The Ship« (1973). Here he reveals the specific combination of individualization and generalization that characterizes the genre of the short short story and makes it useful for classroom use.

Anita Fetzer shows the perspective of **linguistics**. She examines the form and function of small stories in the research fields of sociolinguistics and applied linguistics, presents analyses of small stories in media communication, and adapts the small form to learning scenarios. It becomes clear that small stories are not only an interesting sociolinguistic phenomenon, but provide valuable tools for teaching the grammar of spoken and written English, refining the (mental) lexicon and enhancing discourse competence.

Part B is introduced by **Carola Surkamp**. She explores **mini-sagas** through **drama-based activities**. She realizes that so far suggestions for classroom activities involving mini-sagas have predominantly approached the genre in a written and narrative way. Short narrative texts, however, can also be approached by acting them out. Therefore she examines the questions of where precisely the potential of a drama-based approach to mini-sagas lies, which techniques are suitable for the scenic interpretation of the text, and how drama activities can be prepared and evaluated.

Petra Kirchhoff recommends **Twitterfiction**. First she describes this new literary format, in which authors can use exactly 140 Unicode characters as well as auditive and audiovisual media to tell a story, continue one or just share their ideas with other users. Then she demonstrates that teaching Twitterfiction in English classes is rewarding for many reasons. Students encounter new linguistic forms like acronyms and abbreviations and poetic language in a new format, which conveys immediacy and possibly communicational authenticity. Additionally, Twitterfiction can serve as an excellent starting point for discussing ethical issues in the use of the social media.

Senem Aydin discusses the potential of **picturebooks** to depict the **refugee** experience and raise students' awareness about experiences like persecution, flight and migration. She makes clear that such stories can contribute to students' linguistic, literary, intercultural and affective development. After she has pointed out relevant criteria for selecting suitable stories, she gives us numerous storytelling suggestions for Sarah Garland's picturebook »Azzi in Between«. Her conclusion includes a selected list of recommended picturebooks on migration.

Stephanie Schaidt draws our attention to **metafictive picturebooks**. As this genre constantly transgresses boundaries and plays with literary conventions, it is a rich resource for the EFL classroom. Due to their multilayered nature, metafictive picturebooks can be used with students of different ages and levels of language proficiency. After defining the genre, the author identifies seven metafictive strategies, which she illustrates with numerous examples of self-referential picturebooks. She states convincing reasons why we should use them in the language classroom, and finally suggests several pre-, while- and post-reading activities.

Katrin Stadlinger-Kessel convinces us that students' imagination can be fired by six words, i.e. the shortest short story on record. She presents inspiring suggestions for a 45-minute lesson on **Hemingway's famous short** at an upper-intermediate level. What is most striking here is the contrast between the factual wording of a classified ad and the emotional impact behind it. This is one of the reasons why people find this story so compelling and why it resonates with students, too. For the teacher, there may be another big advantage of dealing with it in class: no preparation is necessary in terms of photocopied materials, the only things needed are a blackboard and chalk.

Bernard Brown claims that short texts are motivating for our students and allow the teacher to integrate them into a well-rounded lesson, using the texts as a »diving board« for other communicative and interactive activities. He suggests several **techniques** such as mazes, corrupted texts, just one word, removing punctuation and capital letters, three-in-one, matching and sequencing, and student created gapped texts.

Part C comprises nine contributions, which demonstrate how certain subgenres of shorties can be employed in the English language classroom:

– Take a closer look at the genre of **proverb**, and its wicked relative, the **perverb**. Students do not only become familiar with the English equivalents of their L1 proverbs, but deepen their knowledge of rhetorical devices, and even create their own perverbs, i.e. anti-proverbs.

– Do you know this **anecdote** about F. D. Roosevelt, the only US President to serve more than two terms, who indulged in some inappropriate small talk at a social function (»I murdered my grandmother«) and received a witty answer from one of his guests? Your students can practise their phatic communication skills, and even promote their power of quick-witted repartee.

– In a similar vein, **urban myths** sound »too good to be true«. Do you believe in the story of the criminals who called the police on their own? Or of the clown statue that only the children see? Urban legends like those are modern folk tales narrating stories which are presumably real, but odd, and supposedly happened to a friend of a friend.

– **Fables** are represented by James Thurber, regarded by many to be America's greatest humorist of the 20th century, and his masterpiece *The Unicorn in the Garden*. In this fable (is it one?), an apparently clever wife tries to send her apparently mad husband to an insane asylum. But, as the saying goes, you shouldn't count your boobies – or chickens – before they are hatched.

– If you were the heroine in the **fairy tale** of *The Princess and the Tin Box*, you would without any doubt fall for the poorest, yet strongest and most handsome prince, wouldn't you? After all, you are an experienced reader who knows that »money can't buy me love«. Modern-day princesses in such fairy tale-fable-parody mash-ups, however, may go for alternative endings – and morals.

– Why not **joke** your way through grammar? After all, grammar is the difference between knowing your crap and knowing you're crap.

– Sparkling humour can also be found in **mini-sagas**, but the two examples treated in this volume deal with rather serious issues (bullying, capital punishment). Students may be encouraged to create their own mini-sagas – or, if 50 words are not enough, some *55 fiction*, or a *drabble* (100 words).

– **Nasreddin stories** are centred on the wise Sufi scholar of the same name, who may – or may not – have lived somewhere in the Middle East in the 13th century. Seeming odd, impudent and absurd at first glance, his actions and statements gradually reveal trickster humour and philosophical wit.

– Finally, **picture books** are exemplified by the wonderful 32-page illustrated text *It's a Book*, which may be read as a delightful manifesto on behalf of print in the digital age. A mouse, a jackass and a monkey discover a new thing – a book! It does not need a mouse or a password, and it cannot text, tweet, or toot. Why not? »Because it's a book«. Apart from enjoying this lovely book on a book, students can consolidate their vocabulary by playing Bingo or doing a vocab relay contest.

»Brevity is the soul of wit«: Let us not imitate Polonius, whose speech is self-contradictory. He wastes plenty of time denouncing the time wasted by rhetorical speechifying. Literary scholars regard Polonius as the least brief and one of the least witty characters in the play, and Sigmund Freud aptly referred to him as »the old chatterbox«. So let's be brief: Enjoy these short contributions on shorties!

A. Theory

Engelbert Thaler

Shorties in English Language Teaching

»We lack the optimism of the 19th century to believe that the world could be captured on 500 pages; that is why we choose the short form« (Jorge Luis Borges). This paradoxical aphorism by the great Argentinian writer draws our attention to the genre of *shorties*.

The following paper attempts to give a few answers to the six W and one H questions:
- What? ▸ Definition
- Why? ▸ Rationale
- When? ▸ Level
- Where? ▸ Venues
- Which? ▸ Types
- What for? ▸ Objectives
- How? ▸ Methodology

1 Definition

> For Sale: Baby Shoes, Never Worn.

This untitled text, which comprises only six words, is said to originate from Ernest Hemingway. It may be the most famous example of *shorties*, i.e. short narrative texts. There is no widely accepted definition of the length of this genre, and the maximum number of words mentioned in various sources varies between 50 and 1,000 words (e.g. Nischik 1997). Although dramatic or poetic texts can, of course, also be very short, they are not subsumed under this term here.

In English, the term *flash fiction* has become established for literary texts of extreme shortness. Prose below 1,000 words is also called sudden fiction, microfiction, micro-story, mini-fiction, skinny fiction, ultra-short stories, short short, postcard fiction, prosetry or short short story. Shorties can look back on a long tradition, from Aesop's fables and Buddhist Zen stories to Vonegut and Cage in the Anglo-American realm, or the Germans Brecht and von Doderer (also cf. Müller in this volume).

2 Rationale

Why should we make use of shorties in our classrooms? To state the obvious, short narrative forms are good teaching material because they are short and narrative. Behind this pleonastic triviality, several benefits of shorties can be detected (Thaler 2008, 2012):

- They are flexible in use.
- They can comfortably be dealt with in a single lesson.
- There is a multitude of forms beyond the classic short story: from traditional simple forms (fairy tales, fables) to more complex narrative genres (short stories) and modern media forms (news stories, hyperfiction).
- The popularity of shorties is increasing. The rise of the Internet has enhanced an awareness of flash fiction, with websites and webzines such as *Flash, Flash Fiction Online* or *Flash Fiction Magazine* being devoted exclusively to this genre. Its succinct and punchy form seems perfectly in line with the online reader, and the ubiquitous hand-held devices are also ideal content delivery systems for short fiction.
- Stories fulfil anthropological, psychological and social needs. Shorties serve a variety of functions: a means of making sense of an individual's experiences, a medium of communication and community, a form of entertainment, a source of solace, a fundamental need (beginning, middle, end). »So while we live with the anxiety that our lives may have one of these key attributes but not the other (they come to an end, but they do not make sense), we comfort ourselves with narratives, which have both these desiderata: they have beginnings, middles and ends, and they make sense« (Toolan 2001: 14).
- They may bridge the gap between the texts in the familiar coursebooks used throughout the first years of instruction on the one hand, and »Literature with a capital 'L'«, i.e. writing of recognized artistic value, on the other.
- A short short story usually has a powerful effect. »Its brevity and condensed resonance make sure it lingers in the mind and heart. It has the power of a poem but with greater clarity and accessibility« (Wells, cited in Burke 2011).
- Shorties are usually characterized by discursive openness. Against the background of the reader-response theory, the aesthetic densification within a minimal space opens up ample scope for diverse reactions and interpretations by the learners. »A short story is a story on which one has to work a long time until it is short« (Vicente Aleixandre).
- Telling stories is an omnipresent phenomenon in everyday life, the media ... and the classroom.

3 Level

At what age should teaching shorties start? Some people argue that literary texts cannot be integrated into the classroom until students have reached a level advanced enough for them to grasp the full meaning. Such an attitude seems restricted if we do not exclude »literature with a small 'l'«, and believe that appreciating literature has to be gradually developed in a long process (Thaler 2008). In particular shorties can be made use of at all levels – from beginners to intermediate pupils and finally advanced students. The age and level of a group has to be considered, of course, in terms of teaching goals, classroom procedures and types of shorties.

Beginners in the primary classroom enjoy short and funny texts such as fairy tales, jokes or picture books. The methods employed must take into account the developmental stage of the learners by including playful and holistic learning, accompanied by movement and music. A technique often tried and tested is storytelling – or at least story-reading. The aim in primary classrooms cannot be a critical analysis of texts but enabling children a first contact with literature, which promotes basic language skills, is fun and enhances the motivation to learn English.

A full understanding of shorties may take place at more advanced levels. All reading techniques can be trained, a profound analysis may be attempted, creative writing and other forms of creating can become more sophisticated. So the initial question may be answered by pleading for »literature for all ages«.

4 Venues

Where can you teach and learn about shorties? The most obvious, yet not the only, place for teaching literature is the classroom, with all the students sitting at their desks and reading the same story. However, one may imagine further options:
- Reading corner (in the classroom)
- Classroom library
- School library
- Literature workshops
- At home
- Public places
- Internet reading
- Mobile-assisted reading

5 Types

Fortunately there is a wealth of diverse forms of shorties for the teacher to choose from (e.g. Allen 1997; Garner 2011; Nischik 1983; Nischik 2005; Reisener 2014; in particular Thomas et al. 2015; Thomas et al. 1992). The following table lists 28 of these types, before some of them are illustrated by sample texts.

Types of Shorties			
jokes	puns	riddles	fairy tales
fables	(anti-) proverbs	quotations / aphorisms	anecdotes
flash fiction	folk tales	urban myths	mini-sagas
Nasreddin stories	letters	epitaphs	ads
failures	prayers	fumblerules	parables
Zen kōans	six-word stories	drabble	twitterature
symbol stories	funny definitions	Murphy's laws	short stories

Table 1: Types of shorties

- Anecdotes

> Lady Astor once remarked to Winston Churchill at a dinner party:
> »If I were your wife I would poison your tea.«
> Without showing any agitation Churchill replied:
> »If I were your husband I would drink it.«

- Mini-sagas

A *mini-saga* consists of exactly 50 words (plus title). If 55 words are required, the text is called *55 fiction*, with 100 words, it is a *drabble*.

> *Like mother, like son*
> 1955
> Dear Mummy,
> I hate this boarding school. Food awful, prefects bully me. Please take me home.
> Love, David
> ---

Dear David,
Nonsense! Chin up. – Mother
1997
Dear David,
I hate this Home. Food awful, nurses treat me like a child. Fetch me immediately. – Mother
---
Dear Mother,
Nonsense! Chin up. – David

- Six-word stories

Strangers. Friends. Best friends. Lovers. Strangers.

- Jokes

On a group of beautiful deserted islands in the middle of nowhere, the following people are stranded:
2 Italian men and 1 Italian woman
2 French men and 1 French woman
2 German men and 1 German woman
2 English men and 1 English woman
2 Irish men and 1 Irish woman
One month later on these absolutely stunning deserted islands in the middle of nowhere, the following things have occurred:
One Italian man killed the other Italian man for the Italian woman.
The two French men and the French woman are living happily together in ménage-a-trois.
The two German men have a strict weekly schedule of alternating visits with the German woman.
The two English men are waiting for someone to introduce them to the English woman.
The two Irishmen divided the island into North and South, and set up a distillery. They do not remember if sex is in the picture because it gets sort of foggy after the first few litres of coconut whiskey. But they're satisfied because at least the English aren't having any fun.

- Puzzles

> What do you say to King Kong when he gets married? (*Kong-ratulations*)

- Anti-proverbs

> All's well that ends. (*Reduction*)
> A barking dog never bites, but a lot of dogs don't know this proverb. (*Supplement*)
> The best things in life are for a fee. (*Substitution*)
> Marriages are made in heaven knows what state of mind. (*Synthesis*)

- Twisted quotes

> Somebody is boring me; I think it's me. (Dylan Thomas)

- Answers to children's letters

> Dear Pamela,
> Santa only brings presents. I'm afraid I cannot take away your baby brother. – Love, Santa

- Fumblerules

> 1. Don't use no double negatives.
> 2. Reserve the apostrophe for it's proper use and omit it when its not needed.
> 3. Do not put statements in the negative form.
> 4. Verbs has to agree with their subjects.
> 5. No sentence fragments.

- Howlers

> Shakespeare was born in 1564, supposedly on his birthday. He lived in Windsor with his merry wives, writing tragedies, comedies and errors, all in Islamic pentameter. Romeo and Juliet are an example of heroic couplet. The next great author, John Milton, wrote *Paradise Lost.* Then his wife died and he wrote *Paradise Regained.*

6 Objectives

Drawing on two dominant paradigms in TEFL, i.e. CLT (Communicative Language Teaching) and ICC (Intercultural Communicative Competence), the goal of teaching literature in class may be called LCC: Literary Communicative Competence (Thaler 2008). Such an objective also applies to shorties and comprises the three domains of knowledge, attitudes and various skills, i.e. reading, understanding (analysing, interpreting), and creating. These three domains as well as the three skills must be seen against the background of communication. They should not be treated as separate dimensions, but foster shorties-based communication and negotiation of meaning.

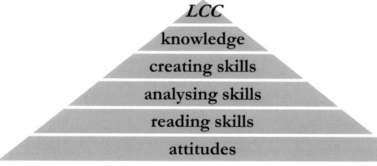

Table 2: LCC

7 Methodology

If the proper text has been selected, and the suitable objectives targeted, the question as to the appropriate method arises.

7.1 Text-adapted Procedure

Each text type and each shorty calls for an individual procedure. For example with jokes, omitting the punch-line during the first reading / telling is to be recommended, asking the students to speculate on the ending. With the inter-cultural joke (see above), only the introductory situation should be read out, the rest is covered, and learners have to propose »educated guesses«; it is funny to realize how close their answers come to the original statements. A general discussion on country-specific stereotypes should round off the sequence.

7.2 Formal-structural Analysis

Even very short texts may be analysed with the help of some of the common literary terms:
- Events, actions
- Characters
- Setting: time, place
- Structure
- Narrator
- Point of view

The limited number of words forces some of those categories to be unspecified or difficult to assess – and these indeterminacies are meant to invite readers to various interpretations.

7.3 Herringbone Technique

A useful technique for analysing a short text is the herringbone technique. This graphic organizer, which resembles a fish skeleton, provides students with a structural pattern by asking of the main idea the six questions: Who? What? When? Where? Why? How?

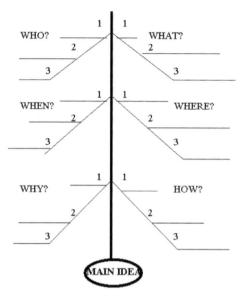

Table 3: Herringbone technique

7.4 Maley's 12 Procedures

Alan Maley (1995) proposes »twelve generalizable procedures for texts« in an inspiring book with the telling name »Short and Sweet«.

Maley's 12 Procedures	
Procedures	*Examples*
1. Expansion	Add one or more sentences
2. Reduction	Remove specified items (e.g. adjectives)
3. Media transfer	Transfer it into visuals (e.g. pictures)
4. Matching	Match text with a title
5. Selection / ranking	Choose the best text for a certain purpose (e.g. inclusion in a teen mag)
6. Comparison / contrast	Identify rhetorical devices common to both texts
7. Reconstruction	Reorder jumbled lines

8. Reformulation	Rewrite in a different mood
9. Interpretation	What does the text not say?
10. Creating text	Use 10 words from the text and write s.th. new
11. Analysis	Study the use of tenses
12. Project work	Use the text for an advertising campaign

Table 4: Generalizable text procedures (Maley 1995)

7.5 Socratic Dialogue

We recently had the pleasure of sitting in on an intriguing classroom lesson held by a visiting teacher on a flash fiction story by Richard Brautigan. Not more than two sentences consisting of only 35 words were analysed by teacher and students for 45 minutes – in an exciting and artful negotiation of meaning interplay full of unexpected twists.

> **The Scarlatti Tilt**
> »It's hard to live in a studio apartment in San Jose with a man who's learning to play the violin.« That's what she told the police when she handed them the empty revolver.

In analogy to the *Socratic Method*, named after the great Greek philosopher Socrates, the teacher in a Socratic dialogue professes ignorance of the subject matter (Wilberding 2014). Such a form of inquiry, which is based on asking and answering questions, intends to stimulate critical thinking and illuminate ideas. Following a dialectical perspective, this technique examines the meaning of a short text by constantly doubting statements put forward by different individuals. It is founded in the conviction that there is no single right answer, all new knowledge is connected to prior knowledge, and asking one question should lead to asking further questions. Eventually such a dialogic approach can bring out deeply rooted conceptions implicit in the interlocutors' comments, and help them deepen their understanding of texts in general – which is the rationale of the so-called *Maieutic (Midwife) Method*.

7.6 Conventions of an Oral Story

Attempting to elicit deep structures, one may also resort to the sociolinguist William Labov, who has proposed six basic rules or conventions of an oral story (cf. Toolan 2001: 148; also see Fetzer in this volume). Studying this pattern may help us to understand how narrators encode information about the world on a personal level.

Oral Telling	
Abstract	What, in a nutshell, is this story about?
Orientation	Who, when, where?
Complicating action	What happened and then what happened?
Evaluation	So what?
Result (resolution)	What finally happened?
Coda	That's it, I've finished and am 'bridging' back to our present situation.

Table 5: Oral telling

7.7 Storytelling

Telling stories is a competence teachers should try to learn and develop – not only when teaching younger learners. In the classroom, storytelling can promote intercultural understanding, offer insights into universal life experiences, develop listening skills, encourage imagination, and promote a feeling of well-being (Thaler 2008).

Not everybody is a born storyteller, but everybody can do it at least for classroom prurposes, and practice makes perfect. The more you tell stories, the better you will become at it, and the more your students – and you – will enjoy it. Master storytellers like Andrew Wright (1995) and Richard Martin (2000) have given us ample advice on how to captivate an audience with the right techniques (also see Ellis/Brewster 2002; Klippel 2000). Several suggestions on selecting the story, remembering the plot, starting the story, using performance techniques, and post-storytelling outcome can be found in Thaler (2008).

7.8 Storywriting

Shorties should not only be read, interpreted and told, but also written. Creative writing can serve a lot of linguistic, communicative, affective and social purposes (Beyer-Kessling 2002: 334; Holtwisch 1999: 418). These positive effects, however, only come into force if the students' imagination is activated by some stimuli, they are informed about types and structures of shorties (genre competence), and they are made aware of writing as a process.

This process of creative writing is divided by Froese (1999: 426 f.) into four phases: inspiration (collecting ideas), incubation (playful experimenting with material), illumination (writing), and verification (editing and publishing). Kieweg (2003) even suggests six stages: idea, structure, writing strategies, first draft, editing, final text. The first version of a text cannot be perfect, but must be edited as to form, content, addressee, or spelling.

It goes without saying that entering the classroom and requesting the students to produce some shorties will not work. Before they can start writing, they must get a stimulus and be put into the proper writing mood. Such a stimulus can take on six forms and trigger off various tasks (Table 6).

Writing Shorties	
Stimulus	*Task examples*
Complete text	Changing persons, times, places
Incomplete text	Enlarging a skeleton text
Missing text	Writing on a title
Text structure given	Parodying a fairy tale
Acoustic stimulus	Listening to music and writing about one's associations
Visual stimulus	Writing a story matching a photo

Table 6: Stimuli for writing shorties

Learners need help in the form of instructions, skeletons or schemes (e.g. Harm 1997) to gradually initiate, process and evaluate their ideas. A few suggestions on how to write flash fiction are offered by Popek (2002), e.g. invent a twist ending, use action verbs, and do cut-cut-cut. Gaffney (2012) emphasizes the following six points:
- Start in the middle.
- Don't use too many characters.
- Make sure the ending is not at the end.

- Sweat your title.
- Make your last line ring like a bell.
- Write long, then go short.

8 Conclusion

To focus on the three major categories of selection, methodology and objectives, a conclusion on shorties may read like this:

a. Genre: The short story has long been accepted as a popular genre in TEFL. It is high time to use shorter short stories and flash fiction as well.

b. Methodology: Teachers should strike a fair balance between analytical and creative procedures.

c. Objective: With the help of shorties, narrative competence with regard to receptive and productive skills should be promoted.

Bibliography

Allen, Roberta (1997). Fast Fiction: Creating Fiction in Five Minutes. Cincinnati: Story Press.

Beyer-Kessling, Viola (2002). Put It in Writing. Kreatives Schreiben im Englischunterricht der Sekundarstufe. Fremdsprachenunterricht 46/2002, 334–339.

Burke, Declan (2011). Flash Fiction: Intense, Urgent and a Little Explosive. The Irish Times Oct 26, 2011. www.irishtimes.com/culture/books/flash-fiction-intense-urgent-and-a-little-explosive-1.631904. (01/01/16)

Ellis, Gail/Brewster, Jean (2002). Tell it Again! The New Storytelling Handbook for Primary Teachers. London: Penguin.

Flash. www.chester.ac.uk/flash.magazine. (01/01/16)

Flash Fiction Magazine. http://flashfictionmagazine.com. (01/01/16)

Flash Fiction Online. http://flashfictiononline.com/main. (01/01/16)

Froese, Wolfgang (1999). Kreatives Schreiben im Englischunterricht der Sekundarstufe I. Fremdsprachenunterricht 6/1999, 424–429.

Gaffney, David (2012). Stories in Your Pocket: How to Write Flash Fiction. The Guardian 14 May 2012. www.theguardian.com/books/2012/may/14/how-to-write-flash-fiction. (01/01/16)

Garner, James Finn (2011). Politically Correct Bedtime Stories. London: Souvenir Press.

Harm, Andreas (1997). My Short Science-Fiction-Horror-Love-Adventure Short Story. Englisch betrifft uns 4/1997, 27–29.

Holtwisch, Herbert (1999). Kreative Textarbeit im Fremdsprachenunterricht und die Bewertung kreativ-orientierter Klassenarbeiten. Fremdsprachenunterricht 6/1999, 417–424.

Kieweg, Werner (2003). Creative Writing. Unterrichts-Materialien Englisch 748E-04/2003, 1–61.

Klippel, Friederike (2000). Englisch in der Grundschule. Berlin: Cornelsen.

Maley, Alan (1995). Short and Sweet. Cambridge: Cambridge University Press.

Martin, Richard (2000). The Strongest of Them All. Berlin: Cornelsen.

Nischik, Reingard (eds.) (2005). Short Stories Universal: Thirty Stories from the English-Speaking World. Stuttgart: Reclam.

Nischik, Reingard (1997). Die Short Short Story im Englischunterricht. Neusprachliche Mitteilungen aus Wissenschaft und Praxis 50:1, 24–28.

Nischik, Reingard (eds.) (1983). Short Short Stories: An Anthology. Paderborn: Schöningh.

Popek, Joan (2002). Flashing Your Setting. www.sjoanpopek.com/writeflash.html. (01/01/16)

Reisener, Helmut (2014). Erfolgsgeschichten und Idealtexte zum Englischlernen. München: Grin.

Thaler, Engelbert (2015). Kurzprosa im Unterricht. Praxis Fremdsprachenunterricht 1/15, 7–9.

Thaler, Engelbert (2012). Englisch unterrichten. Berlin: Cornelsen.

Thaler, Engelbert (2009). Method Guide. Kreative Methoden für den Literaturunterricht. Paderborn: Schöningh.

Thaler, Engelbert (2008). Teaching English Literature. Paderborn: UTB.

Thomas, James/Shapard, Robert/Merrill, Christopher (eds.) (2015). Flash Fiction International: Very Short Stories from around the World. New York: Norton.

Thomas, James/Thomas, Denise/Hazuka, Tom (1992). Flash Fiction: Seventy-two Very Short Stories. New York: Norton.

Toolan, Michael (2001). Narrative: A Critical Linguistic Introduction. London: Routledge.

Wilberding, Erick (2014). Teach Like Socrates: Guiding Socratic Dialogues and Discussions in the Classroom. Austin: Prufrock Press.

Wright, Andrew (1995). Storytelling with Children. Oxford: Oxford University Press.

Timo Müller

Short Short Stories: Literary Perspectives

Very short forms of narration are almost ubiquitous in popular culture, as literary scholars noted from an early point. From radio commercials to music videos to snapchat posts, very short narratives have become more widespread and at the same time more condensed. The digital natives of the early twenty-first century are used to 15-second videos and 140-character posts, which they take in at the rate of dozens or even hundreds a day (Nischik 2005: 208). The literary history of »shorties« reaches back far beyond the advent of the mass media, however, and in some national literatures the short short story is an established genre of its own. The Spanish *microrrelato* is particularly popular in Latin America and has been studied extensively by scholars, but Turkish and Arab literatures are familiar with the genre as well (Lagmanovich 2006; Siles 2007; Andres-Suárez 2010). In English, the short short story has been overshadowed by the more traditional genres (poem, drama, novel) but also by the short story, which emerged in the United States and has remained highly popular there. As a result, the short short story went unrecognized by scholars until the late twentieth century and continues to receive scant attention.

It has been given several names, including »sudden fiction« (Shapard and Thomas 1986), »flash fiction« (Thomas, Thomas and Hazuka 1992), and »micro fiction« (Stern 1996). The oldest and arguably most fitting term, however, is »short short story.« First used by the naturalist writer Frank Norris in 1896, the term is almost as old as »short story« itself, which was popularized by the influential scholar Brander Matthews from the 1880s onward (Nischik 2005: 90; Nischik 1997: 25). It has prevailed over other versions and is widely used in German scholarship as well, most notably in *Short Short Stories: An Anthology* (1983) and *Short Stories Universal* (2005), both edited by Reingard Nischik. These anthologies provide a useful overview of the genre and feature examples from various periods and national literatures. The latter is a Reclam edition and thus especially convenient for classroom use. The discussion in the following is informed by examples from all of these collections but will focus on the formal features and the didactic potential of the short short story in general. After a brief historical overview, it situates the short short story in relation to other genres, discusses the reading strategies it demands, and illustrates these findings by the example of Joseph Bruchac's story »The Ship« (1973).

1 A Short Short History

Like its older sibling, the short short story emerged out of precursors like the fable, the parable, the anecdote, and the sketch in the early nineteenth century (Current-García 1985: 1–24; Stern 1996: 16; Chantler 2008: 39). While the term itself dates from the end of the century, many earlier writers already published narratives that can be classified as short shorts. Among the precursors frequently mentioned in scholarship are the ancient Roman satirist Petronius (of *Satyricon* fame), the nineteenth-century French writers Charles Baudelaire and Guy de Maupassant, and the Russian realist Nikolai Gogol (Stern 1996: 17; Evenson 1997: 8; Chantler 2008: 39). In the English-speaking world, early examples include Edgar Allan Poe's »The Oval Portrait« (1842), the shortest of his tales, which contains a yet shorter tale embedded in the frame narrative; Stephen Crane's »A Tent in Agony« (1892) and »The Mesmeric Mountain« (1892); Kate Chopin's »The Story of an Hour« (1894); Mark Twain's humoristic anecdotes; and many of O. Henry's stories, such as »Lord Oakhurst's Curse« (1883) and »Heart and Hands« (1903). Crane's work has been singled out by the scholar Brian Evenson for anticipating the modern short short story (1997: 8), but arguably the stories by Poe and Chopin more closely approximate the dramatic development and psychological depth we expect of stories today.

In the modernist period, the literary avant-garde shifted the focus from plot and content to language and form. This relieved the short short story of its gravest problem to date: the lack of space to develop a plot that might qualify as a story. Leading modernists like Ernest Hemingway and Virginia Woolf shaped their style in very short forms: Hemingway in the telegraphs and newspaper articles he wrote as a foreign correspondent for American newspapers, Virginia Woolf in lyrical prose pieces and in the early stories she published together with her husband. Hemingway's first published book, the collection *in our time* (1924), consisted of vignettes that became the so-called interchapters of the better-known revised version, *In Our Time* (1925), where they offer snapshots of motifs that appear in the longer stories as well. The longer stories are not only written in Hemingway's characteristic paratactic style, but some are short enough to count as short short stories in their own right. One of them, tellingly entitled »A Very Short Story,« runs only to about 600 words.

The examples mentioned so far, however, are ultimately isolated cases. The breakthrough of the short short story did not come until the postmodernist period, which discarded requirements like realistic character development and a coherent plot that had left earlier writers dissatisfied with the genre. If postmodernism is characterized by its rejection of »grand narratives,« as the theorist Jean-François Lyotard argued in his period-defining study *The Postmodern*

Condition (1979), the short short story becomes attractive not least because it is by definition a small narrative. And indeed, the short short story turned out to be a fitting medium for the postmodernist aesthetics of fragmentation, experiment, wordplay, and resistance to closure. The American writer Robert Coover became one of the pioneers of the genre from the 1970s onward, especially as editor of »Minute Stories,« a special issue of the journal *TriQuarterly*, which appeared in 1976. The very title of the issue suggests that the stories collected here no longer take »a half-hour to one or two hours« to read, as Edgar Allan Poe wrote in his much-quoted definition of the short story (1984 [1842]: 572), but a few minutes at most. With a different pronunciation (»minute« rhyming with »suite«), the title also suggests that the stories are extremely small or short. The two words of the title thus tell at least two different stories about the contents of the volume. This sort of wordplay was widely used among postmodernists to enrich their texts with as many meanings as possible. In the terminology of the time, this strategy undermines the presence and stability of meaning by multiplying the signifieds (associations) evoked by each signifier (word).

The short short story thus became the counterpart to another favorite genre of the postmodernists, the sprawling meganovel. If Thomas Pynchon's *Gravity's Rainbow* (1973) and David Foster Wallace's *Infinite Jest* (1996) multiply their signifieds by expanding and fragmenting the text, the authors of »Minute Stories« arrive at this goal by means of condensation. The postmodernist avant-garde was not the only factor in the boom of the short short story at the time, however. As daily newspapers and gossip magazines found themselves in competition with television and other mass media after World War II, they adjusted to the shortened attention span of consumers by cutting down the length of texts. A considerable market thus appeared for mass-produced short short stories. In a study of all stories published in the women's magazine *Good Housekeeping* between 1965 and 1970, the cultural historian Bruce Lohof found that all of these stories rely on the same plot structure. They combine a series of standardized »modules«: hero is introduced; villain is introduced; confrontation between« hero and villain takes place; villainy is transformed into heroism; conflict is resolved (1982: 82). The gender and the ethnic and social background of both hero and villain vary, Lohof notes, although the hero in most cases is a white Protestant young man. The underlying plot structure remains the same and guarantees the reader's familiarity with the story as well as a satisfactory conclusion (1982: 81–93). Lohof also found that the stories were expected to contain a moral lesson while entertaining readers at the same time, which places them in the tradition of Horace's *prodesse et delectare*, one of the oldest aesthetic norms in Western literary history.

The distinction between avant-garde and popular literature has gradually been leveled in recent decades, and the short short story has been part of this trend not least because it lends itself to online publication. The digital realm has further shortened readers' attention spans, and many popular communication platforms (Twitter, Snapchat, Instagram) encourage brevity, as their very names announce. The short short story conforms to these new reading habits and fits a variety of online publication venues, including blogs, in which a large portion of online literary debate takes place. These venues not only allow writers to make their work available immediately and free of charge, but it provides opportunities for instant reader response and for discussion between reader and writer. Online publication seems to have secured the status and the productivity of the short short story. Given the differentiation into longer print formats and shorter digital formats observable in current literary publishing, the short short story is likely to migrate almost entirely into the digital realm.

2 Genre Typologies

The short short story can usefully be defined by its relationship to other genres: to other forms of narrative literature, but also by its position in between narrative literature and poetry. Within narrative literature, the boundaries of the short short story are marked by the classic short story on one side and by very short forms such as anecdote, aphorism, joke, parable, riddle, and sketch on the other. The first of these distinctions, between short story and short short story, is based solely on length, though scholars are divided on where exactly to set the boundary. Some put the outer limit of the short short at 2,500 words (Howe 1982: x) while others cap it at 1,000 or 1,400 words (Nischik 2005: 191; 205). The latter suggestion is preferable from a typological perspective since the former includes many classic short stories and thus loses its distinctive function. Some scholars set a minimum length at 150 or 250 words (Nischik 1997: 24; Wright 2014: 344) to distinguish the short short story from other very short forms, while other scholars require structural elements like a plot that unfolds in time, »be it a temporal or logical sequence of actions or events, an evolving dialogue, or an intellectual or emotional development« (Nischik 1997: 24; cf. Nischik 2005: 203–204; Wright 2014: 335). Ultimately, both a minimum length and a plot seem necessary to distinguish the short short from anecdotes, jokes, and sketches in particular. »Extreme brevity will degenerate into epigrammatism,« as Poe already noted in his definition of the »short prose tale,« and texts of fewer than 150 words invariably run that risk (1984 [1842]: 572). A plot is an indispensable element of storytelling and enables a fairly sharp distinction from short prose types that do not require elements such as setting, character, conflict, and resolution (cf. Evenson 1997).

The scholar Ashley Chantler has recently pointed out that the short short story calls into question another generic distinction within narrative fiction: that between collections of short short stories and novels (2008: 39–48). Since the turn of the twentieth century a number of writers have published thematic collections of short shorts that read like chapters of a novel. Chantler's examples include Barry Yourgrau's *A Man Jumps Out of an Airplane* (1999), Dan Rhodes's *Anthropology and a Hundred Stories* (2000), Dave Eggers's *Short Short Stories* (2005), and David Gaffney's *Sawn-Off Tales* (2006). Novels have long operated with modular chapters that can be arranged in various orders, and some experimental novels, such as Sandra Cisneros's *The House on Mango Street* (1984), resemble collections of vignettes more than traditional realist narratives. The difference to collections of short shorts is not always obvious, especially in a postmodernist context.

Another typological level on which the short short story can instructively be discussed is the distinction between narrative and poetry. In the nineteenth century these genres were clearly distinguishable because poetry was defined by its use of verse and meter. (The verse epic was regarded as a poetic genre from Romanticism at the latest, as was the ballad.) In the modernist period the distinction began to be questioned from both sides. On one side, the definition of poetry was extended to include short prose texts like Hemingway's vignettes or the pieces collected in Gertrude Stein's *Tender Buttons* (1914). On the other side, narrative texts began to be composed in a tight, evocative language of the sort previously associated with poems. The most influential proponent of this approximation of poetry and narrative was the American poet Ezra Pound, a pioneer of modernism in both England and the United States. In Pound's opinion, most of the texts that were passing for poetry in the early twentieth century were not actually poems but prose texts chopped into verses. The poetics he developed in response to such inept versifying was modeled not on conventional lyrical categories but on the »unspeakably difficult art of good prose« (2005 [1913]: 95). From now on both genres, poetry and narrative, were measured by very similar standards. Many of Hemingway's stories use a skillfully composed, extremely condensed language that lives up to the best poems in the literary tradition; inversely, Pound wrote short poems that, while they benefit from their verse structure, can also be read as samples of aesthetically wrought prose. His imagist poems are among the best-known results of this innovative approach:

In a Station of the Metro

The apparition of these faces in the crowd;

Petals on a wet, black bough.

(Jones 1972: 95)

Alba

As cool as the pale wet leaves

    of lily-of-the-valley

She lay beside me in the dawn.

(Jones 1972: 96)

Not everyone was open to such innovation in the modernist period, and more conventionally-minded contemporaries coined the term »prosetry« for poetry that was not sufficiently lyrical in tone (Withington 1931: 279). The term has never been widely used but it acquired a positive connotation from the 1970s on, when spoken-word artists and experimental poets began to appreciate it for capturing the generically hybrid quality of their work (McFadden 1978; Jacobs 1993).

The role of the short short story in the approximation of narrative and poetry has been discussed by several scholars, including well-known figures like Franz Stanzel and Irving Howe. In an essay titled »Textual Power in (Short) Short Story and Poem,« Stanzel approaches the genre question from a reader-response perspective and argues that modern short prose pieces »make demands on their readers which are closer to those of poetry than to those of novelists« (1990: 22–23). He points out that many writers of short shorts originally emerged as poets, for example George Bowering, Richard Brautigan, and Langston Hughes. Stanzel presupposes a certain type of short fiction, however, which values meditation over action and lyrical over prosaic language. This makes his argument a circular one, and it leads to categorizations that do not necessarily apply to stories other than those he discusses (1990: 28). Howe offers a more stringent analysis of the relationship between the short short story and the lyric poem. In his introduction to the anthology *Short Shorts: An Anthology of the Shortest Stories*, he argues that »the short short is to other kinds of fiction somewhat as the lyric is to other kinds of poetry. ... The lyric does not seek meaning through extension, it accepts the enigmas of confinement. It strives for a rapid unity of impression, an experience rendered in its wink of immediacy.« Like the lyric poem, Howe suggests, the short short story is marked by »overfocussing« and creates a sense of immediacy despite its temporal extension (1982: xiii–xiv).

Other scholars have defended the distinction between short short story and prose poem. John Gerlach convincingly argues that stories direct our attention to character, conflict, and the spatiotemporal conditions in which they evolve, whereas most prose poems describe a momentary situation and transmit a mood, atmosphere, or reflection. »[I]f we take a character as reflector upon an idea,« he concludes, »we have a poem; if we take him as a character who happens to be thinking, we have a story« (1989: 82–84). Ultimately, however, the short short story might be most interesting for typological discussions because of its very in-between position, which allows it to challenge and modify genre boundaries. A short short story can adopt traits of an anecdote, a meditation, or a vignette; it can borrow from the riddle, the fable, or the dictionary entry. It thus exposes and subverts conventional beliefs about the content, reception, and authority of these genres (Evenson 1997: 9). More importantly, by combining traits of various narrative and poetic genres, the short short has inspired a remarkable range of approaches. In the early 1980s, Howe distinguished four main types of short shorts, which he defined by plot structure: »One thrust of incident«, »Life rolled up«, »Snap-shot or single frame«, »Like a fable« (1982: xv–xvi). Two decades later, the afterword to the abovementioned anthology *Short Stories Universal* identifies almost a dozen types or modes of very short fiction: realist, postmodern, surreal-hyperrealist, psychological-impressionist, humorist-satirical, social-critical, parabolic, essayistic, lyrical, mythological, and regionalist (Nischik 2005: 200). The list indicates that short shorts cover a broad range of topics and cultural backgrounds, which makes them a substantial resource for classroom use.

3 Reading Strategies

Hemingway already knew that extreme reduction of plot and setting creates a specific reading experience. The memorable image he found for this insight was that of the iceberg. His stories were like icebergs, he said, in that their meaning was largely »below water«: it was not spelled out by the text but shimmered underneath, creating a sense of vast depths to be sounded out beneath the surface (1932: 192). Short short stories necessarily reduce plot and setting, and if well written they can resemble Hemingway's icebergs. The iceberg principle requires a sensitive yet analytical approach on the part of the reader, who needs to recognize subtle allusions and measure the emotional depths of the story. In other words, it requires the sort of 'close reading' that has been the standard approach of literary criticism since the mid-twentieth century. Close reading entails careful examination of the setting, time frame, characters, language, and plot structure of a story. It often requires several readings of the text under examination, going back and forth to identify crucial elements and examine their interconnections. The reader-response pattern (*Appellstruktur*) of the short short story thus approximates that of poetry (Iser 1970). Both genres direct the reader's attention not so much to progress and causality—the main concerns of conventional narrative—as to the formal organization of the text. Beside the inevitable temporal dimension of reading a text from beginning to end, they demand a spatial reading as well (Frank 1945: 225–235). Readers need to examine the whole of the story to understand its individual parts, and they need to analyse how exactly each part contributes to that whole. The shorter the text, moreover, the more important the individual word or phrase, especially when words are used figuratively—for example as symbols or metaphors—and thus carry additional meanings and implications (cf. Stanzel 1990: 23).

Beside close reading, however, the short short demands a very different reading strategy as well. Like parables, fables, and other short forms, it encourages generalization, in the sense of wide applicability. The shorter the narrative, the less specific the information it provides, which explains why many short forms carry a sense of the exemplary, representative, and allegorical (Nischik 1997: 26). If the short story classically traces an individual's psychological, moral, or biographical development, the short short is often interested in development as well but without individualizing the character. In Howe's words, »circumstance eclipses character, fate crowds out individuality, an extreme condition serves as emblem of the universal.« As a result, short shorts do not create an »impression of life,« as most other fiction does, but »an impression of an *idea* of life« (1982: xiii).

The contradictory reader response demanded by the short short—close reading on the one hand, abstraction on the other—makes the genre useful for didactic purposes because it acquaints students with the basic strategies of textual analysis. An illustrative example is Native American writer Joseph Bruchac's »The Ship« (1973). The story is 303 words in length and thus a short short by any definition; it features individualized characters, specific settings, and a coherent plot, which distinguishes it from other very short forms of narration. The story can be divided into two parts, each of which ends with a sudden recognition on the narrator's part. Here is the first part:

> I was a small boy. We were on board a steamship on a resort lake. As we went by the shore the captain would announce to the passengers details about the cottages on the banks.

> »This is the estate,« squawked the loudspeaker, »of the owner of the Algonquin Motor Lodge.« A hugely windowed mansion with great pillars.

From the docks and the steps of boathouses people waved as we passed.

»This is the summer home of the President of the Albany Savings Bank.«

I lifted my small arm and waved back.

»This is the summer home of …«

»You notice they don't tell where the poor people live,« said a man wearing a worn blue shirt to the woman and the child behind him. I noticed the woman's clothing was out of date and uncomfortable looking. I noticed the woman's hair was thinning and her face seemed to be worn thin like sandstone by wind. Then I noticed she was my mother. (59)

The very first sentence of the story introduces the opposing tendencies of individualization and generalization that pervade the story and set the scene for the first moment of recognition. The narrator introduces himself as an individual (»I«) but at the same time as a generally representative figure (»a small boy«). The »we« of the second sentence continues this tension as it can be read either narrowly (denoting the boy's family, for example) or widely (referring to everyone on board the ship). The story does not offer any exposition beyond these two sentences, so that it continues to hover between the individual and the general. The question of what the pronouns mean, of who they refer to, in these sentences can alert students to the importance of close reading. It also introduces the question of narrative perspective, which is kept in the foreground by the disconnection between the captain's announcements and the boy's thoughts: he is interested in the people on the shore, not in the houses the captain is pointing out. Narrative perspective becomes crucial in the last paragraph quoted here, where the boy's perception becomes the dramatic action of the story. This pattern is repeated in the second part of the story:

I kept waving at the people on beaches and on floats, in boats and in the water. Then a little girl went by in a huge power boat driven by a man whom I knew must be her father. I waved … but she didn't wave back.

I looked up at my mother. »Little girl didn't wave.«

»She didn't see you.«

»But I wave to her. Why can't she …« My mother interrupted my words with a weary wave of her hand.

»Look around you!« she said.

I looked. The boat was full of mothers and children. They leaned over rails and dangled through portholes. All around were children my age, younger, older, in varying degrees of happiness and sorrow, good clothing and bad, clean faces and dirty. And each of them was waving, thinking the returned wave from the shore was for themselves alone.

Once again the boy's perception keeps shifting to the foreground and takes center stage in the recognition that ends the story. Where the first recognition scene is about individualization—the boy recognizes an anonymous woman as his mother—the second is about de-individualization as the boy recognizes himself to be an anonymous member of a crowd. This final recognition becomes possible because the boy adopts the perspective of the girl in the other boat, that is, an outside perspective on himself. Tracing the play of narrative perspective is another exercise in close reading and, like the conclusion of the story, confronts readers with the subjectivity of (their own) perception. A third layer that requires careful attention is language. Students can be asked to point out grammatical errors in the boy's narrative, such as »whom I knew must be her father« and »But I wave to her«, and to reflect on the contribution this language makes to the story: it emphasizes that the perspective is a child's and introduces the motif of fallibility that prepares the recognition scenes. The double meaning that the word »wave« acquires in the maritime setting might have a predictive function as well: just as the tranquil, artificial »resort lake« fails to produce impressive waves on the water, the girl's wave comes to seem artificial to the boy.

Yet the story also requires the opposite reading strategy, namely a look at the text as a whole: at its structure, its genre conventions, and the general import of its message. The text draws on the three-part structure typical of fairy tales, fables, and other types of de-individualized short narrative. The captain points out three homes on the shore, and it is after the third announcement that the boy experiences his first recognition. On a higher structural layer, the text can be divided into five phases: the exposition in the first paragraph, the boy's waving to people on the shore, the first recognition scene, the boy's waving to the girl, and the second recognition scene. This way of looking at the story highlights not only the parallels between the waving and recognition scenes but also the mounting tension between the boy's perception and that of the other people in the story. In the first waving scene the boy is part of a crowd waving to another crowd; in the second he is part of a crowd waving to an individual, which stresses the de-individualizing dynamic of the story. The plot thus mirrors the tendency toward generalization that characterizes the genre of the short short story. Together with the generalizing title (»The Ship«), this plot dynamic shifts the story toward a related genre, the parable, which uses allegorical figures to illustrate a generally applicable moral. In this context the Native American background of both author and text point to another interpretive approach to the story. The reference to the »Algonquin Motor Lodge« indicates a history of appropriation and exploitation beneath the story that, like the underwater part of Hemingway's icebergs, gives additional resonance to the boy's unflattering perception of his mother and to the tension of privilege and inferiority that characterizes his encounter with the girl. This tension also indicates that Bruchac's story is not a parable after all. The recognition scenes have an individual as well as a general significance, and the subjectivity of individual perception is a leitmotif. This enables students to empathize with the boy and imagine themselves in his place.

»The Ship« thus illustrates the specific combination of individualization and generalization that characterizes the genre of the short short story and makes it useful for classroom use.

Bibliography

Andres-Suárez, Irene (2010). El microrrelato español: Una estética de la elipsis. Palencia: Mensocuarto.

Bruchac, Joseph (1983). The Ship. 1973. In: Nischik, Reingard (ed.) Short Short Stories: An Anthology. Paderborn: Schöningh, 59–60.

Chantler, Ashley (2008). Notes towards the Definition of the Short-Short Story. In: Cox, Ailsa (ed.) The Short Story. Newcastle: Cambridge Scholars, 38–52.

Current-García, Eugene (1985). The American Short Story before 1850. Boston: Twayne.

Evenson, Brian (1997). Introduction: The Short-Short Story. In: The Short-Short Story. Spec. issue of Cimarron Review 119, 8–9.

Frank, Joseph (1945). Spatial Form in Modern Literature. Part 1. Sewanee Review 53:2, 221–240.

Gerlach, John (1989). The Margins of Narrative: The Very Short Story, the Prose Poem, and the Lyric. In: Lohafer, Susan/Clarey, Jo Ellyn (eds.) Short Story Theory at a Crossroads. Baton Rouge: Louisiana State UP, 74–84.

Hemingway, Ernest (1924). in our time. Paris: Three Mountain Press.

Hemingway, Ernest (1925). In Our Time. New York: Boni & Liveright.

Hemingway, Ernest (1932). Death in the Afternoon. New York: Scribner's.

Howe, Irving (1982). Introduction. In: Howe, Irving/Howe, Ilana Wiener (eds.) Short Shorts: An Anthology of the Shortest Stories. Boston: Godine, ix–xvii.

Iser, Wolfgang (1970). Die Appellstruktur der Texte: Unbestimmtheit als Wirkungsbedingung literarischer Prosa. Konstanz: Universitätsverlag.

Jacobs, Bruce A. (1933). Cathode Ray Blues: Poetry and Prosetry. Baltimore: Tropos Press.

Jones, Peter (ed.) (1972). Imagist Poetry. London: Penguin.

Lagmanovich, David (2006). El microrrelato: Teoría e historia. Palencia: Menoscuarto.

Lohof, Bruce (1982). American Commonplace: Essays on the Popular Culture of the United States. Bowling Green, OH: Bowling Green State UP.

Lyotard, Jean-François (1984). The Postmodern Condition: A Report on Knowledge. 1979. Trans. Geoffrey Bennington and Brian Massumi. Minneapolis: U of Minnesota P.

McFadden, David (1978). On the Road Again. Toronto: McClelland and Stewart.

Nischik, Reingard (1997). Die Short Short Story im Englischunterricht. Neusprachliche Mitteilungen aus Wissenschaft und Praxis 50:1, 24–28.

Nischik, Reingard (eds.) (1983). Short Short Stories: An Anthology. Paderborn: Schöningh.

Nischik, Reingard (eds.) (2005). Short Stories Universal: Thirty Stories from the English-Speaking World. Stuttgart: Reclam.

Poe, Edgar Allan (1984). Review of Twice-Told Tales by Nathaniel Hawthorne. 1842. In: Thompson, G.R. (eds.) Edgar Allan Poe: Essays and Reviews. New York: Library of America, 569–577.

Pound, Ezra (2005). A Few Don'ts by an Imagiste. 1913. In: Rainey, Lawrence (eds.) Modernism: An Anthology. Malden, MA: Blackwell, 95–97.

Shapard, Robert/Thomas, James (eds.) (1986). Sudden Fiction: American Short Stories. Salt Lake City: Smith.

Siles, Guillermo (2007). El microrrelato hispanoamericano: La formación de un género en el siglo XX. Buenos Aires: Corregidor.

Stanzel, Franz K. (1990). Textual Power in (Short) Short Story and Poem. In: Nischik, Reingard/Korte, Barbara (eds.) Modes of Narrative: Festschrift für Helmut Bonheim. Würzburg: Königshausen, 20–30.

Stern, Jerome (eds.) (1996). Micro Fiction: An Anthology of Really Short Stories. New York: Norton.

Thomas, James/Thomas, Denise/Hazuka, Tom (eds.) (1992). Flash Fiction: Very Short Stories. New York: Norton.

Withington, Robert (1931). Some Neologisms from Recent Magazines. American Speech 6:4, 277–289.

Wright, Frederick A. (2014). The Short Story Just Got Shorter: Hemingway, Narrative, and the Six-Word Urban Legend. Journal of Popular Culture 47:2, 327–340.

Anita Fetzer

Small Stories: Theories and Applications

The goal of this chapter is to examine the form and function of small stories in the research fields of sociolinguistics and applied linguistics, to present analyses of small stories in media communication, and to adapt the small form and its communicative functions to learning scenarios for teaching the grammar of spoken English.

1 Small Stories

Narratives have been examined in literary studies and in the heterogeneous field of (socio)linguistics. They are distinguished with respect to issues of quantity, that is longer narratives and small stories, issues of quality, that is who are the heroines and heroes, and issues of style, that is literary style or (in)formal spoken and written styles. Small stories are a particular kind of oral narrative, which has been examined in Applied Linguistics and Discourse Analysis (e.g. Georgakopoulou 1997; Ribero/Bastos 2004), in the Ethnography of Speaking (e.g. Hymes 1996), and in Social Psychology and Sociolinguistics (e.g. Coates 2003; Labov 1972; Norrick 2000).

The discursive turn in arts and humanities as well as in the social sciences has also had an impact on various fields of linguistics. It has promoted an analysis of language structure and language use going beyond the questions of grammaticality, acceptability and appropriateness. What is more, it has led to the explicit differentiation of spoken and written language, as is reflected in the description of the rules and regularities of spoken English in standard reference grammars, such as *A Comprehensive Grammar of the English Language* (Quirk et al. 1985) or the *Longman Grammar of Spoken and Written English* (Biber et al. 1999). Thus, it is not only the clause which is described as grammatical or ungrammatical, but also discourse in spoken and written modes, and discourse for specific purposes. The change of perspective has also altered the focus of grammatical analyses, where grammaticality is no longer of prime importance. Instead, »language patterns above the sentence« (Widdowson 2004: 3) are examined considering the conditions for discursive well-formedness and its appropriateness in context.

In line with linguistic tradition and linguistic methodology, the unit of investigation of this chapter, that is small stories, will be analysed with respect to its form and function.

1.1 Form

In everyday discourse, small stories are an (optional) part of a whole, which is not necessary for discourse to be felicitous, in speech-act-theoretic terms. As regards their form, small stories are embedded in discourse and form an autonomous sequence. As regards their structure, necessary conditions for a stretch of talk to count as a small story are (1) a reference to a single past – or hypothetical future – event, (2) a temporal sequence of events represented in at least two clauses which are temporally ordered and coded in past tense; alternatively they may refer to the future, (3) a point (raison d'être), (4) relevance of personal experience to the ongoing event, and (5) its reportability / tellability.

The influential Labovian model (Labov/Waletzky 1967) proposes the following components of oral storytelling: *abstract, orientation, complicating action, evaluation, resolution* and *coda*. These components form the building blocks of a prototypical small narrative.[1] The following table systematizes them and accommodates their sequential organization:

1. Abstract	A brief summary of the substance of the small story.
2. Orientation	Relevant contextual information about time, place and participants.
3. Complicating action	Thematic development coded by a sequence of events that move the story forward. Each event is separated from the other by a temporal juncture.
4. Evaluation	The focus of the narrative, which is usually realized with evaluating clauses. The evaluation may be strong, moderate or weak, and it may be realized explicitly or implicitly.
5. Resolution	The final action and conclusion.
6. Coda	The teller relates the narrative to the here-and-now and spells out its relevance to the here-and-now.

Table 1: Labovian model

These prototypical building blocks of small stories entail further aspects, for instance the number of characters and the questions whether they are represented in a mono- or multilithic manner and whether they are silent, single- or multi-voiced, and the social status and gendered identities of heroines or heroes.

---

1   Johnstone (2001) distinguishes between *stories,* i.e. narratives with a point, and *narratives,* i.e. talk which represents events in the past.

Ochs/Capps (2001) have supplemented the rather formal model of Labov/ Waletzky (1967) with a more open-ended perspective capturing the qualitative aspects of narrativity and narratives, which are put to practice in the oral production of narratives, such as *tellership*, which highlights the interactive nature of storytelling, *tellability*, which entails newsworthiness, *embeddedness*, which refers to the here-and-now of the interaction, *linearity*, which refers to a linguistically and extra-linguistically ordered sequence of events, and *moral stance*, which is functionally equivalent to the building block of evaluation within a moral order. The more flexible structuring of small narratives allows for multiple forms, which also include future-oriented or hypothetical content. As a consequence, small stories may have past-orientation and thus deal with breaking news, or they may be oriented towards the future and narrate projections. Breaking news refers to very recent events ('this morning', 'last night') and are communicated to share both content and emotional involvement. Projections refer to the telling of near-future events. They are fabrications of the future, which may become »rehearsals for future actions« (Georgakopoulou 2007: 150).

In everyday communication small stories go beyond »recapitulating past experience by matching a verbal sequence of clauses to the sequence of events which actually occurred« (Labov/Waletzky 1967:20). They thus enable communicators to connect the here-and-now of the interaction and the participants with what has been relevant then and what may become relevant in the future. Small stories thus fulfil important social and interpersonal functions, such as signifying solidarity, bonding, offering advice or preparing for future action. They are used strategically to support the construction of discursive identities and to secure common ground, as is going to be examined in more detail below.

1.2 Function

Narratives in general and small stories in particular have been examined across various fields of application, such as classroom discourse, therapeutic interaction, institutional discourse and media discourse. They have an important function in the construction of discursive identities, such as gendered identities, expert identities or ordinary-people identities. In educational and therapeutic contexts, they are used to contextualize advice, for instance by saying »when my sister encountered similar learning problems, she would keep a learning diary and that has helped her immensely to improve her academic standing. You know she would write every single detail down, just to make herself aware of what she was doing with those 24 hours every single individual has at their disposal« rather than »do not waste your time« or »you must learn to budget your time«. Small stories – or one or more of its constitutive parts – may also be used to support one's argument by placing it in a more persuasive context, such as »learning diaries can be used by learners of modern languages at school, and they are also used at universities where they are called 'module diaries'«, thus illustrating the impact of the argument and strengthening its pragmatic force. In mundane everyday discourse, they are frequently used to express intimacy with others, while at the same time construing solidarity with self. Small stories report of personal experience, usually with the teller as the protagonist, making sense of experience of what is happening to her/him and around him/her.

Small stories have been described as past-oriented, reporting about events, which have happened before. More recently, especially because of the influence of social media, their future-directedness has been acknowledged, reporting on more hypothetical scenarios embedded in upcoming discourse. Against this background, Goffman (1974) explicitly relates the construction of discursive identities to the dramatization of past experience, which is assigned the status of ›relevant/noteworthy experience' supplemented with a more or less explicit moral stance of self and others. Future-direct small stories are used to rehearse anticipated critical situations and thus provide personalized problem-solving strategies. In positioning theory, Davies/Harré (2001) point out the importance of stories and story lines, in particular as stories play an important role in our social lives and in the construction of coherence in discourse and across discourse. Through narratives, people can reconstruct past experience and make various facets salient in interaction.

In the following, the form and function of small stories anchored to the personal spheres of life is examined in the context of media communication, which is public by definition.

2 Small Stories in Context

Small stories have been described as personal narratives anchored to the individual's private domains of life. Media discourse is public discourse, and with the advent of social media, it has become even 'more' public, as programmes or relevant excerpts may be communicated and forwarded to a selected audience, if not to all members of social-media networks, who may then forward those excerpts to other users.

In the media, small stories are frequently used to initiate a debate about a particular issue or contribute to the debate, such as discrimination, equal pay or empathy. As such, they are intended to initiate follow-up sequences, in which the face-to-face audience in the studio, or the mediated audience with their digital gadgets, comment on the story by evaluating it or by providing other small stories relevant to the topic. The uncoupling of (shared) time and (shared) space in media communication and the communication through a medium has consequences on (1) how the small story is told and followed-up in the media, and on (2) how the comments are linguistically realized and whether other semiotic codes are involved. In general, evaluations are expressed in a more explicit manner in mediated communication in the social media, and the protagonist's face is threatened more directly.

Small stories have been told in the media across various contexts: they have been told in political debates, in science programmes or in sitcoms. In all of those settings, public speakers take on the role of a public teller of a 'private story'. In general, the private story paves the ground for a discussion of recent events, or the announcement of breaking news. The following excerpt from the party-political address 'The opportunity society' by the then Prime Minister Tony Blair at the Annual Labour Conference 2004 serves as an illustration of the form and function of small stories in political discourse.[2] It starts with the prototypical opening section, in which the audience is addressed directly and in which the speaker thanks them for the welcoming applause ('Conference, thank you very much for that'):

> *Conference, thank you very much for that that welcome and before I start my speech, I want to express our condolences to the latest British casualties in Iraq and I want on behalf of all of us to express our support and solidarity to Ken Bigley and all the Bigley family. They are in our thoughts and prayers.*

[APPLAUSE APPLAUSE APPLAUSE]

> **Right and now for the speech. So here we are again,** *my toughest week yet, since the last one, until the next one. An important speech, I've got a lot to say,* **in fact** *I bumped into Rodney Bickerstaff who's written a few good speeches in his time*

[CHEERS]

> *and I told him I was I was worried this speech is going to be to*

[HECKLING AND BOOING]

---

2   To facilitate readability, the transcription of the speech is in accordance with orthographic standards. The reaction of the audience is printed in [square brackets], the small story is underlined, THE STORY WITHIN THE STORY IS UNDERLINED AND FORMATTED IN SMALL CAPS, and *relevant linguistic cues are printed in bold italics.*

Thank you

[HECKLING AND BOOING]

That's that's fine sir, you can make your protest, just thank goodness we live in a democracy and you can

[APPLAUSE APPLAUSE]

Actually I got a bit confused there, I thought no one boos Rodney Bickerstaff, *it's ridiculous.*

[LAUGHTER]

Anyway I was telling you I bumped *into Rodney* **he said he said don't worry** *about the length of the speech and he showed me he showed me this cutting,* **and I quote** »Chief Mangosuthu Buthelezi, leader of Inkatha, was yesterday on the seventh day of a speech to the Kwazulu Legislative Assembly.

[LAUGHTER]

His speech began on the Friday the twelfth, broke for the weekend, continued the following Monday, paused again last Friday, and resumed again with the ominous announcement that the introduction was now over.«

[LAUGHTER]

So so here we are facing *the possibility ...*

Public speeches, in particular political speeches transmitted through ordinary media and/or through official websites or social media, display a variety of linguistic cues which bracket their constitutive units, that is opening and closing sections, topical sections or side sequences. In Tony Blair's extract above, the opening section is delimited from the 'actual speech' (or: topical sections) by the discourse marker[3] **right** and the untensed metapragmatic comment *and now for the speech*, anchoring the speech to the here-and-now with the adverb of time *now* and the adverb of place **here**. The discourse marker **so** indicates the final move of an argumentative sequence, which co-occurs with the collective self-reference **we** with an inclusive referential domain. The politician thus sets

---

3   Discourse markers are indexical devices which have procedural, but no conceptual meaning (cf. Jucker/Ziv 1998). They are used to bracket units of talk, signalling transitions and boundaries, and to communicate interpersonal meaning and attitude, for instance.

the stage for what is to follow and comments on the relevance of the topical part of the speech that is to come. Before the topical part is delivered, however, the opening part is bracketed with metacomments on the speech (*An important speech, I've got a lot to say*) and with another discourse marker, *in fact,* which signals another digression, this time in the shape of a small story.

In line with the structuring of small stories the politician starts with a very brief abstract referring to the teller, that is the politician himself, and the protagonist of the small story, Rodney Bickerstaff (*I bumped into Rodney Bickerstaff*). This is followed by an orientation (*Rodney Bickerstaff has written a few good speeches in his time*) and a complicating action (***and I told** him **I was I was worried** this speech **is going** to be to*) which remains elliptical because the teller gets interrupted by members of the audience and needs to comment upon the interruption. However, the social context makes it quite clear that the politician is worried about the length of the speech he is about to deliver. The section on the complicating action is taken up again, which demonstrates the relevance of that part to small stories, with a quotation from the protagonist of the small story, introducing a small narrative with another protagonist (CHIEF MANGOSUTHU BUTHELEZI) within the small story to be told.

The evaluation within the small story is also quite explicit (***don't worry** about the length of the speech*) and communicated by protagonist$_1$ (Rodney Bickerstaff), and the resolution is presented in form of another, embedded small narrative referred to by *this cutting* which the teller then reads out (***and I quote** »CHIEF MANGOSUTHU BUTHELEZI, LEADER OF INKATHA, WAS YESTERDAY ON THE SEVENTH DAY OF A SPEECH TO THE KWAZULU LEGISLATIVE ASSEMBLY. HIS SPEECH BEGAN ON THE FRIDAY THE TWELFTH, BROKE FOR THE WEEKEND, CONTINUED THE FOLLOWING MONDAY, PAUSED AGAIN LAST FRIDAY, AND RESUMED AGAIN WITH THE OMINOUS ANNOUNCEMENT THAT THE INTRODUCTION WAS NOW OVER«*). This is followed by the final part of the embedded small story, the coda, introduced by the discourse marker *so*, and another reference to the here-and-now by the adverb of place *here* and the collective self-reference *we* (***So so here we are facing** the possibility*), relating the story to the face-to-face audience and other mediated audiences, spelling out its relevance to the present political situation. The teller of the small story and its embedded small narrative uses the communicative form to break the ice and align with the audience, who laugh at the story and with the politician. In that context, laughter counts as a form of applause.

As for the grammar of telling small stories, the use of adverbs, especially of time and place, is important. This also holds for the use of discourse markers and the linguistic realization of self- and other-references. The use of tense and aspect is also very interesting, especially if it deviates from standard use. For instance, the strategic use of progressive and non-progressive aspect, and perfective and non-perfective aspect relate the narrative content to the here-and-now, supporting the dramatization of the story line: non-progressive forms signify chains of action while progressive forms foreground unbounded action; deictic tense and personal pronoun shifts in reported speech signal ordinariness, and non-deictic tense and personal pronoun shifts in reported speech underline the relevance of the reported speech or thought to the here-and-now.

Small stories are also told in dyadic political media discourse. The following excerpt stems from a political interview, in which the interviewee, Charles Kennedy, uses the small story to support his argument in favour of political changes. This time, there is no explicit abstract but only the discourse marker *well,* which brackets the small story. The orientation slot is introduced with a self-reference and a verb of cognition (*I remember*) and a description of the setting *when decimalisation came in,* which is taken up (*at the time*) in the complicating action (*my grandparents at the time shaking their heads and saying that this marked the end of civilisation as we know it*). The evaluation and resolution are merged and bracketed with the discourse marker *now* and are also rather explicit, but indeterminate (*maybe it did, maybe it didn't*), while the coda is introduced with the contrastive discourse marker *but* contrasting it from the indeterminate evaluation:

> **Well** I I remember **you know** when decimalisation came in. **Erm and I remember** my grandparents at the time shaking their heads and saying that this marked the end of civilisation as we know it. **Now** maybe it did, maybe it didn't. But I don't think anybody today would seriously argue that we go back to a system of internal currency which is pounds shillings and pence, would they?

This small story is very brief and its sequence of actions is orderly. What is different to the prototypical small story is the merger of the abstract and orientation, and resolution and coda. As regards the grammar of story telling, there are a few deictic and temporal shifts, and a few non-shifts (***this*** marked the end of civilisation as we ***know*** it), underlining the relevance of the narrative content to the here-and-now. The small story is used to underline the politician's argument and construe solidarity with the audience, as is reflected in the marker of common ground **you know**.

In the following, the form and function of small stories are adapted to the contextual constraints and requirements of teaching English as a foreign/second language.

3 Applications

The oral form of small story offers a lot of possibilities for implementing it into the SLA (second/foreign-language acquisition) classroom. It allows for a structured approach to teaching (1) the grammar of spoken English, including interaction management, style, register and prosody, (2) interpersonal functions, for instance the expression of social hierarchies or of solidarity, and (3) the strategic use of pragmatic intensification, that is boosting or attenuating the pragmatic force of a speech act, or of a move in an argumentative sequence.

Telling small stories in the SLA classroom is connected intrinsically with teaching the grammar of spoken English, which requires an explicit distinction between written English and spoken English as described by Leech/Svartvik (1994: 17 f.):

> »In writing we work with sentences. But it is often hard to divide a spoken conversation into separate sentences. Part of the reason is that the speakers rely more on the hearers' understanding of context, and on their ability to interrupt if they fail to understand. Also, in 'getting across' their message, speakers are able to rely on features of intonation, which tell us a great deal that cannot be rendered in written punctuation.«

The different transmission systems and their defining conditions and particularized features can be systematized as follows:

Spoken – fragmentary and involved	Written – integrated and detached
Transmitted by sound waves, originated in speaking and received in hearing	Transmitted by letters and other visible marks, produced in writing and received in reading
Fast, almost instantaneous production and understanding	Time to plan, revise, check and rewrite – and time to read, reread and ponder
Language, including gesture and gaze	Formatting and fonts, Spacing
Chunking	Punctuation devices
False starts Pauses (silent/voice-filled) Short forms	

Context-dependent meaning	Context-independent meaning
Pronouns	Proper nouns
Demonstratives	Definite articles
General nouns	Indefinite articles
Elliptical clauses	Non-elliptical clauses
Yes/no-answers	Full answers
Higher frequency of	**Higher frequency of**
Speaker self-references	Noun phrases
Private verbs	Participles
Routine formulae	Passives
Discourse markers	Complex structures
Vagueness/hedging	Explicitness
Repetition	Attributive adjectives
Redundancy	Higher density of information

Table 2: Spoken vs written English

Communication is both process and product. It involves a production side, that is speaking and writing, and a reception side, that is hearing and reading. However, there is more to communication than just the production and reception of a communicative contribution. Rather, that very basic exchange needs to be expanded by the accommodation of communication-as-a-process, as is reflected in the receiver's uptake, in and through which s/he demonstrates her/his comprehension of the speaker's contribution. The uptake is functionally equivalent to the production of a new communicative contribution, relating it with the previous one with the help of discourse markers, pronouns and demonstratives and the appropriate use of tense and aspect. The use of those cohesive devices is necessary for both spoken and written communication.

Spoken and written English need to be taught by comparing and contrasting the two modes, considering in particular that »[n]ormal speech is processed in real time and is transitory, leaving no trace other than what we may remember. (...) Writing, on the other hand, takes longer to produce and can be read not just once but many times. Writing leaves a permanent record« (Leech/Svartvik 1994: 10). Against this background, spoken and written English do not have different grammars, but the shared English grammar is used differently in the two channels, as has been systematized above. The grammar of spoken and written English can be applied to teaching small stories in the SLA classroom, where it may need to undergo context-dependent particularization, as is examined in the following.

The discursive form of small story offers a number of learning scenarios and particularized tasks for students of English. It can be used to improve receptive skills, e.g. listening comprehension of Standard English and/or of selected varieties of English, or listening comprehension supported by visual input. It can also be used to improve the students' productive skills by students producing small stories in spoken or written formats, either individually or as joint production. Small stories can be approached from a holistic perspective, focussing on the entire story, and they can be used to produce or comprehend one or more of their constitutive parts, such as abstract, orientation section, complicating action, evaluation, resolution or coda:

- As for the abstract, the skill of presenting precise information can be refined, in particular the use of tense and aspect, i.e. simple forms vs. progressive and perfective forms. Apart from that, the linguistic realization of information can be compared and contrasted for spoken and written modes, and can be varied with respect to recipient design, for instance children, university students or academics. Alternatively, the abstract may be composed for different media outlets (printed media, social media).

- As for the orientation section, similar learning scenarios may be used as for the abstract section. Additionally, the ordering of adverbials can be integrated regarding the positioning of time, location, circumstance and manner adverbials. Closely connected with word order is the distinction between grammatical and pragmatic word order, and thematic progression and information management. Another very important aspect is the differentiation between progressive and non-progressive forms, and perfective and non-perfective forms, and their preferred usage in spoken and written modes[4]. The differentiation between extra-linguistic 'time' and linguistic 'tense' can also be addressed, pointing out the communicative function of historic present, or of deictic non-shift regarding demonstratives, adverbs of time and place or personal pronouns.

- As for the complicating action, the strategic use of tense and aspect, pragmatic and grammatical word order, as well as deictic and non-deictic shifts will be the most important issues. Teachers need to point out that rules and

---

4   The distinction between progressive and non-progressive aspect is very important for German learners of English, who tend to over-use progressive forms. Here, tables with different contexts of use can be identified together with the learners, analysing different English (spoken and written) texts.

regularities of the grammar of spoken and written English can be exploited to communicate particularized meaning, for instance creating tension, highlighting relevant information and expressing involvement or detachment. As with the abstract and orientation section, strategies for the selection of adverbs and adverbials as well as demonstratives can be refined.

- As for the evaluation, the semantics of evaluative expressions, in particular the use of pragmatic intensification, the selection of appropriate adjectives and nouns, and the difference between denotation and connotation require explication. Additionally, learners need to be made aware of different degrees of formality, that is a more informal or conversational style and a more formal or academic style. This holds for both the written and spoken modes.
- As for the resolution, learners need to be familiar with strategies for differentiating between relevant and not-so-relevant information, and they need to find out how 'relevance' can be 'done with words'. Here, a thorough examination of the communicative functions of routine formulae, which underline the relevance of a communicative contribution over which they have scope, would be in order, for instance, the identification of cues such as 'what is more important', 'now', 'guess what', or 'to underline/stress X'. This also holds for the strategic use of tense and aspect, and for pronouns and adverbs anchored to the here-and-now. The syntactic phenomenon of pragmatic word order, that is fronted constituents in which important information is encoded, would also need to be addressed at this stage.
- As for the coda, summarizing information, presenting it in a logical and succinct order will be one of the main issues to be investigated. Furthermore, connecting information and discourse, that is building bridges by encoding relevant cohesive ties would be another desideratum, and – last but not least – the formulation of the coda would need to be adapted to mode (spoken or written), style (formal or informal), to the audience and to the discourse of which the small story is a constitutive part.

As for the small-story-as-a-whole, students may produce them individually or opt for joint production. The advantage of the latter lies in the negotiation-of-meaning processes involved which may contribute to raising their language awareness as regards grammar, the lexicon, style and discursive competence. This also goes for the reception format. Analogously to the production process, comprehension tasks may be performed individually or as a joint endeavour. Another important issue is the explicit accommodation of the addressee(s). By producing small stories for different types of addressees and for different purposes, learners will expand and refine their linguistic, sociolinguistic and discursive competences. Should different cultural contexts be accommodated in the production and comprehension of small stories, their intercultural competence will also be enriched.

Small stories do not occur in isolation, but are parts of longer stretches of discourse, such as everyday talk, gossip, political discourse, therapeutic discourse or educational discourse. Because of their embeddedness in context, small stories need to be delimited from the embedding discourse. This is usually done by the strategic selection of a reporting frame (Mushin 2004) with a 'telling' verb of communication (e.g. tell, say, remember) as framing device. Again, learners may be provided with the opportunity to analyse different communicative functions for verbs of communication encoded in the progressive or perfective aspect, and for verbs of communication encoded in simple forms.

Small stories are encoded in a temporal sequence of events adhering to strict linearity, its point or raison d'être needs to be referred to, and it needs to be reportable. The latter can – again – be connected explicitly with style and register, with the recipients, and with culture and cultural taboos. Small stories in the SLA classroom can be used from a process-oriented perspective for individual or joint text production, or for individual or joint listening comprehension. From a product viewpoint, they can be used to produce other stretches of discourse, which may embed the small story under investigation. To preach and practice the grammar of spoken English, small stories can be performed in role plays, their linguistic realization can be formatted in such a manner that the stories vary systematically in accordance with story-internal features (e.g. characters and their voices, heroes or anti-heroes, gender and genderlect, ethnicity and ethnolect, social status and social dialect) as well as with contextual variables, such as recipient design (e.g. education, ethnicity, age, institution) and outlet (printed media, social media, telephone conversation, face-to-face interaction).

4 Conclusion

Small stories are an interesting sociolinguistic phenomenon, which have a long oral-narrative research tradition, considering their forms and communicative functions, in particular interpersonal functions. Small stories provide valuable tools for teaching the grammar of spoken and written English. They can be used to teach grammar in an integrated, more applied frame of reference, concentrating on syntax and the differences between grammatical and pragmatic word order, and on the semantics and pragmatics of tense and aspect. Small stories are also of importance with regard to expanding and refining the (mental) lexicon, accommodating style and register as well as the huge field of evaluative terms. As regards discourse competence, they can be of immense importance to enlarge the learners' knowledge about cohesive ties and discourse connectivity, and for the grammar of spoken English, the strategic use of discourse markers.

Bibliography

Biber, Douglas (1988). Variation across Speech and Writing. Cambridge: Cambridge University Press.

Biber, Douglas/Johannson, Stig/Leech, Geoffrey/Conrad, Susan/Finegan, Edward (1999). Longman Grammar of Spoken and Written English. London: Longman.

Coates, Jennifer (2003). Men Talk: Stories in the Making of Masculinity. Oxford: Blackwell.

Davies, Bronwyn/Harre, Rom (2001). Positioning: the Discursive Production of Selve. In: Wetherell, Margaret/Yates, Simeon J./Taylor, Stephanie (eds.) Discourse Theory and Practice: A Reader. London: Sage, 261–271.

Fetzer, Anita (2015). Appropriateness in Context. Bulletin suisse de linguistique appliquée, 13–27.

Georgakopoulou, Alexia (1997). Narrative Performances: A Study of Modern Greek Storytelling. Amsterdam: John Benjamins.

Georgakopoulou, Alexia (2007). Thinking Big with Small Stories in Narrative and Identity Analysis. In: Bamberg, Michael (ed.) Narrative – State of the Art. Amsterdam: John Benjamins, 145–154.

Goffman, Erving (1974). Frame Analysis. New York: Harper & Row.

Hymes, Dell (1996). Ethnography, Linguistics, Narrative Inequality. Toward an Understanding of Voice. London: Taylor & Francis.

Johnstone, Barbara (2001). Discourse Analysis and Narrative. In: Schiffrin, Deborah/Tannen, Deborah/Hamilton, Heidi (eds.) The Handbook of Discourse Analysis. Oxford: Blackwell, 634–649.

Jucker, Andreas/Ziv, Yael (eds.) (1998). Discourse Markers. Descriptions and Theory. Amsterdam: John Benjamin.

Labov, William/Watzlewski, Joshua (1967). Narrative Analysis: Oral Versions of Personal Experience. In: Helm, June (ed.) Essays on the Verbal and Visual Arts. Seattle: University of Washington Press, 12–44.

Labov, William (1972). Language in the Inner City. Philadelphia: University of Philadelphia Press.

Leech, Geoffrey/Svartvik, Jan (1994). A Communicative Grammar of English. London: Longman.

Mushin, Ilana (2004). Evidentiality and Epistemological Stance. Narrative Re-Telling. Amsterdam: John Benjamins.

Norrick, Neal R. (2000). Conversational Narrative. Storytelling in Everyday Talk. Amsterdam: John Benjamins.

Ochs, Elinor/Capps, Lisa (2001). Living Narrative: Creating Lives in Everyday Storytelling. Cambridge: Harvard University Press.

Quirk, Randolph/Greenbaum, Sidney/Leech, Geoffrey/Svartvik, Jan (1985). A Comprehensive Grammar of the English Language. London: Longman.

Ribero, Branca/Bastos, Cabral (2004). Telling Stories in two Psychiatric Interviews. AILA Review 18, 58–75.

Widdowson, Henry (2004). Text, Context, and Pretext. Critical Issues in Discourse Analysis. Oxford: Blackwell.

Data

Blair, Tony (2004). The Opportunity Society.
http://news.bbc.co.uk/2/hi/uk_news/politics/3 697 434.stm. (08/12/2015)

Kennedy, Charles (2001). Challenge the Leaders.
http://news.bbc.co.uk/news/vote2001/hi/english/question_time/newsid_1 247 000/1 247 695.stm. (08/12/2015)

B. Methodology

Carola Surkamp

Exploring Mini-Sagas through Drama Activities

1 What is a Mini-Saga?

In order to explain the genre of the mini-saga, looking at the following meta-mini-saga can be helpful. It details the basic characteristics of the genre while using the actual structure of the genre itself:

Mini-Sagas

A mini-saga is a story of exactly fifty words,

no more, no less.

It should tell a complete story

with a beginning, a middle and an end.

It should make a point,

have some drama or some psychological truth in it.

It must, in fact, be a saga in miniature.

MACHA PUMPHREY

Huntingdonshire Writers' Group

(in Proges 2007a: 5)

According to this definition, a mini-saga is a short short story which consists of exactly fifty words, features a tripartite structure with a beginning, a body and an end, focuses on a single event or one moment and has a punchline, twist or surprise ending. Furthermore, mini-sagas begin in medias res and make limited use of adjectives and adverbs. The limited number of words that can be used to tell the story restricts the author to the story's essential points.[1]

Given the density of the plot as well as the fact that many aspects can only be hinted at, mini-sagas exhibit a great number of gaps. The reader has to fill those gaps by using his or her imagination. The (few) characters, for example, are not described in detail and the reader barely learns anything about their emotions. The place and time of the story and the concrete situation in which the narrated

---

1 Cf. Redhead in Proges (2007a: 170): »With a limitation of fifty words, you shouldn't really find any adjectives. And if you put an adverb in, it is usually because you have chosen the wrong verb.« For further information on the history of the mini-saga since its appearance in 1982 as well as on its high order of popularity in Great Britain, cf. Proges (2007b: 165 ff.) and Siebold (1998: 17).

event takes place are usually only implied, too. What is more, many mini-sagas have an open ending. The following mini-saga incorporates all these features and has indeed a surprising ending:

The Canal Path Murders
She could hear the sounds of heavy footsteps as
she hurried down the lonely canal path after dark.
A man's hand grabbed roughly at her sleeve
and she spun round, her legs weak with fear.
He was holding a gun and stared stupidly at her.
»You dropped this«, he said.

MARGARET HODGSON
Telegraph Media Group Limited
(in Proges 2007a: 136)

The indeterminacy and incompleteness of the genre usually cause different readers to imagine the situational embedding of the story, as well as the age and appearance of the characters and their respective relations to one another in a rather divergent way.[2] It is for this very reason that mini-sagas carry great potential for the foreign language classroom. The »world in miniature« (Proges 2007b: 177) which is created within mini-sagas by means of minimalist devices virtually calls for a reflection and a mental dwelling on this world beyond the actual reading process (cf. ibid.). Mini-sagas encourage a meaningful exchange, when learners negotiate their understanding of the story and their interpretations of the subtext. The genre asks for an oral or written embellishment of the stories in order to fill its gaps. To read and work with mini-sagas thus leads to a kind of natural 'opinion gap situation' which can result in authentic verbal interaction in class (Siebold 1998: 19). Furthermore, the characteristics of the genre function as a motivation for learners to draft their own texts. The

---

2   Cf. the inventor of the mini-saga, Brian Aldiss, who uses the different readings of jurors to illustrate the extent to which the interpretations of a mini-saga can vary: »Without betraying any secrets, [...] Maggie Gee and Fay Weldon immediately claimed it was a story of child abuse, whereas Victoria Glendinning understood it as a wife listening to her unloved husband coming up to bed. I saw it as the story of an old woman, her grandparents long dead. Ambivalence can be a virtue, as here. Whichever way it is interpreted, it remains a sad, beautiful and haunting story« (in Proges 2007a: 171 f.). The relevant mini-saga in this case was »Survival« by Bridie Richie: »The door clicked open – as it always did. She lay still, pretending to be asleep. As the footsteps approached, she took what remained of her mind into the wardrobe at the end of her bed where her grandparents were waiting – their arms outstretched to take her dancing amongst the wildflowers« (printed in Siebold 1998: 19).

experience of being able to write an entire story with only fifty words can be inspirational and motivating.

As a result, suggestions for classroom activities involving mini-sagas have predominantly approached the genre in a written and narrative way. Siebold, in particular, has focused on mini-sagas in reference to foreign language teaching and learning. In several articles he has suggested a variety of activities for working with the genre, including the composition of a prologue and/or epilogue to the mini-saga, inventing a new character within the story, telling it from the perspective of another character, rewriting the text as a letter or a picture story, or authoring an own mini-saga (cf. Siebold 1998: 23, Siebold 2015: 7).

Something which has widely gone unnoticed so far, however, is that short narrative texts can also be approached by acting them out. This article examines the questions of where precisely the potential of a drama-based approach to mini-sagas lies, which techniques are suitable for the scenic interpretation of the text and how drama activities can be prepared and evaluated.

2 Why Use Drama Approaches with Short Narrative Texts?

Drama-based techniques have an inherent potential for the foreign language class (cf. Surkamp/Elis 2016). The concept of playful learning activates the learners and challenges them to use the foreign language. Since the verbal action is embedded into a concrete situation which demands certain speech behaviour and which structures the course of the conversation, drama activities promote the speaking competence of learners (cf. Elis 2015). Furthermore, the process of language acquisition does not only demand the active usage of verbal means of communication, but also of nonverbal ones. Nonverbal elements convey meaning and can assist speech production even if purely verbal means are lacking (cf. Surkamp 2014).

With regard to literary education, one major advantage of drama-based techniques is their ability to make literature an experience. Through their enactment, texts become vivid. This is not only a cognitive matter; rather, the stimulation of different senses and activities eminently challenges the learners emotionally and creatively, too. Scenic methods promote learners' awareness of their own experiences, values, sensations and fantasies. Eventually, this can lead them to use these insights for the process of in-depth text comprehension and interpretation, for example through empathising with the characters.

This approach is called 'staged interpretation' ('szenische Interpretation') and was developed by Ingo Scheller (2004). The aim is not to perform a text in a theatre-like setting. Instead, Scheller's method focuses on the use of drama

approaches with the aim of interpreting a literary text through the actions of
the learners. Literary understanding is embodied in the holistic, sensory processing of the text by learners acting out individual passages or scenes, i.e.
by bringing them to life. As playing is a rudimentary human need, the use of
scenic methods also increases the learners' motivation in general. Additionally,
the combination of speaking and movement creates a relaxed and concentrated
learning environment.

For these reasons, drama-based techniques are predominantly applied in
class when working with dramatic texts. Especially because plays are not pure
reading texts, but rather scripts for performances, it is suggested that they be
treated in a different way than narrative or lyric texts in class. Given that dramatic texts mainly consist of dialogues and that the events are presented directly
through the characters acting, it seems reasonable to analyse the text through
an active and productive approach.

Nevertheless, drama-based techniques can also be applied productively when
working with narrative texts. They can, for example, serve to help pupils work
out the character constellation of a story by means of a freeze frame. Methods
like the 'hot seat', where pupils take the roles of certain characters, facilitate
the reconstruction of the characters' different perspectives. A role-play can help
learner to visualise, experience and, thus, understand the conflicts between the
characters.

With regard to mini-sagas, which are told in a minimalistic manner, scenic
methods can support pupils in grasping the events in an easier way, for example by visualising the scene that is depicted in the story. What is more, the
enactment requires the learners to fill gaps in the narration. They need to de-
termine the situation in which the events are taking place. This way, they specify place and time (often not indicated in the mini-saga) and contextualise the
scene. The prologue can be staged or the learners can continue the story after
the open ending of the mini-saga. The characters' inner world of emotions and
thoughts, which is usually only implied in mini-sagas, can also be explored by
expressing it implicitly via gestures, facial expressions, intonation, etc. Similarly, the elaboration of the characters' lives 'outside' of the narrated story is up to
the learners during the reception of mini-sagas: by means of scenic approaches
and, for example, further invented dialogues, the learners allot the characters
a biographical background, a certain behaviour and even individualised body
language.

All in all, the learners are given the opportunity to visualise their own reading
of the story and use more forms of expression to do so than only the verbal one.
Role play is always a form of interpretation. The manner in which the characters say something, the choice of facial expressions and gestures as well as the

way their interaction with the other characters is performed, are substantial indicators of how the different characters and their actions within the story are understood by the participants in the role play.

Since a large number of mini-sagas are told in dialogues, they almost inevitably demand enactment. Proges (2007b: 176) distinguishes between 'action stories', in which an event is narrated, and 'quote stories', in which the event is depicted through a dialogue. Especially the 'quote stories' are suitable for the application of drama-based techniques. Similar to dramatic texts, they present learners with the opportunity to test the effects of facial expressions, gestures and body language as well as paralinguistic phenomena such as intonation, rhythm, pitch, pace and breaks in a dialogue. Aldiss emphasises the fact that mini-sagas hold oral features: »Ideally I like reading them aloud [...] because you should feel the words are coming out in the right places. It's part of the old oral tradition« (cited in ibid.: 172, FN 11).

3 Warm-up

Before beginning the actual scenic work with the text, pupils should be prepared for the use of drama techniques. Although the study of dialogic mini-sagas may prompt acting and playful learning in itself, acting has to be practised so that it can be used as an efficient method in foreign language classes. In addition, pupils first have to be motivated to act. Therefore, a short warm-up phase is recommended.[3]

The warm-up phase serves the purposes of activating learners who are tired from sitting, of promoting their capacity for concentrating and taking things in, and of creating a relaxed atmosphere. Dramatic warm-up exercises such as interactive games – for example the human knot or free fall (cf. Nünning/Surkamp 2010: 176 f.) – also aim at building the necessary trust between pupils for cooperating later in the actual work with the text, and at creating a group climate of communal endeavour in which teachers themselves should also become involved as participants. Ideally, the warm-up exercises should be related to the subsequent dramatic work and help pupils prepare for it in terms of content.

The main aim of scenic work with respect to mini-sagas is to animate the characters – about whom the learners do not learn much from the text itself – and to specify the setting in which they act. Therefore, it seems reasonable to prepare the use of movements in the room. In addition, learners should prac-

---

3   Suggestions for warm-up games can be found in Maley/Duff (1982) and Nünning/Surkamp (2010: 175–179).

tise the ability to employ gestures, mime and their voices as diverse means of expression, for example in order to illustrate emotions or their relationships to other characters or the situations the characters are in at the moment.

A suitable exercise for this purpose is, for example, 'a walk around the room' (*'Raumlauf'*), during which the pupils do not talk but are asked to walk around and adapt their movements to specific instructions such as (cf. Nünning/Surkamp 2010: 177):

> Move as if walking through mud. / Move as if walking barefoot over hot sand on the beach. / Walk as if being followed and feeling nervous. / Move very slowly and without making any noise. Etc.

In another activity, pupils have to guess emotions (cf. ibid.). Three pupils work together, decide on a feeling that can be associated with one of the characters of the text, and present this feeling in front of the whole group through gestures and facial expressions. The depiction of the respective feeling should be done in such a way that the first pupil shows, for example, slight anxiety, and the other two pupils try to increase the emotional expression of anxiety accordingly (for example by a more striking facial expression and/or greater physical exertion). The task for the rest of the pupils is to guess the emotion shown.

A good preparation for a focus on non-verbal as well as paralinguistic communication is an activity called 'line improvisation' (cf. ibid: 178 f.). In this exercise, two pupils face each other a few meters apart. In turns, each takes one small step towards the other, placing one foot directly in front of the other. Both are given a word or phrase that they say at every step, taken from a mini-saga, for example. Pupil A can say: 'I' and pupil B: 'You'. They are instructed to recite these words or phrases with varying degrees of emphasis, volume (conversational level, shouting, whispering), tonality, speed, etc. In doing so, the learners develop a feeling for subtleties such as the importance of vocal expression in acting and for the change in meaning implied by a change in emphasis. Thereby, basic communication patterns, such as 'to ingratiate oneself', 'to give a cold shoulder', 'to plead', 'to reject', 'to insist' or 'to oblige someone', to name but a few examples, are rendered audible (cf. Müller 1992: 368). When the two pupils meet, they switch roles or change perspectives: stepping backwards and retreating step by step, they now recite their partner's word or phrase in a different way with each step.

An advanced exercise that also focuses on body language is the mute or pantomimic representation of a mini-saga, depending on the situation that is depicted in the story. In groups, pupils can prepare the presentation of a mini-saga through pantomime. Within the framework of the mime, they convey information about external events and internal processes, about feelings and attitudes entirely through facial expressions, gestures and movements. The other pupils function as spectators relying solely on the visible signs. After the performance, the audience expresses what non-verbal information they were able to capture and how they interpret the situation and the relationship between the characters.

4 Dramatic Reading Activity

In a next step, learners do a dramatic reading activity. Dramatic reading requires more preparation than reading aloud. Readers must agree on which text passages they will read aloud and on which other signs they will use to present their story: audible signs like intonations and pauses as well as visible signs such as physical movement and postures (walking, standing, and sitting), positioning in space (standing or sitting near to or far from each other, with or without eye contact, with or without body contact) in addition to the design of the setting.

For this activity only a few or implied acting techniques are required (cf. Frommer 1995: 19). The setting is roughly set up or improvised, for example with tables and chairs, and the scenic situation is hinted at by the entrances and exits, the movements, ways of walking and gestures of the performers reading (with text in hand). The spatial arrangement of the characters is crucial. In contrast to reading aloud in which the speakers are randomly seated in the classroom, the readers in a dramatic reading are seated in specifically assigned places. Through this meaningful arrangement of the readers and the choreography of their movements, the space acquires its own system of signs. That way, the exercise makes the spatial dimension of a performance visible and tangible (cf. ibid.: 20).

With the aid of a dramatic reading activity, learners become aware of the fact that mini-sagas are texts with several gaps that can be filled individually. For this purpose, different pairs or groups of learners should enact the very same mini-saga in specified contexts and concrete roles. Since all of these performances will turn out to be different – depending on which actor/actress casts for which role, how they will develop their characters in detail and which atmosphere the depicted situation will be ascribed –, the comparison of various productions of one and the same mini-saga also presents an opportunity for aesthetic learning. On the one hand, it becomes evident that the transformation of a text into a different medium, in this case from a written text to a production, always constitutes an interpretation. On the other hand, the activity shows that the readers of a literary text do not only extract meaning. Instead, they draw on personal experiences, connotations and personal knowledge in the process of comprehending a text. In order to come to an individual understanding of the text they use these underlying patterns in the sense of a 'top-down processing'.

Such an approach suits the following dialogical mini-saga »Girl Talk – A Case History«, taken from the anthology by Progres:

> »Funny thing, SADS,« she said.
> I thought a moment. »Don't you mean SIDS?«, I ventured.
> »No, SADS – Sudden Adult Death Syndrom.
> Happened to a friend of mine once – she died really suddenly just as she was leaving her husband. Very stressful event.«
> »Heart attack?« I asked.
> »No, he shot her.«

> Heather Barker
> Littleborough
> (in Proges 2007a: 93)

Precisely because the characters in this text are not described any further, it is necessary to fill in some of the information gaps. The dialogue, for example, could take place between an older and a younger person or between a very cheerful and a rather sullen one. As a scaffold, learners could be offered cards containing ideas for different situations and character constellations,[4] for example:

- The speakers are cold and distant. They talk to each other, but they don't have anything to do with each other.
- One speaker is very old and speaks slowly with a trembling voice. The other speaker is much younger and tries to support the elderly person.
- The speakers are totally out of breath, as if they had to run fast. They speak fast and feel pursued.
- The speakers only whisper, as if they have to hide and are anxious about being caught.
- One speaker is in a very good mood and sometimes laughs his/her head off. The other speaker feels embarrassed and tries to calm the other person down.
- The speakers are show-offs and speak in a highly ironic and mocking way.
- The speakers are rappers and chant their text rhythmically.
- The speakers are in love. They are flirting with each other.

---

4 Further tips on 'dramatic reading activities' can be found in Grieser-Kindel et al. (2006: 57 ff.).

5 Acting out a Mini-Saga

Subsequent to the different preparatory activities, learners then perform a role play of an entire mini-saga. In Proges (2007a), there are some so-called 'quote stories', which are highly suitable for this purpose, for example »Feed the Birds« (ibid.: 9), »Class Distinction« (ibid.: 11) and »Like Father, Like Son?« (ibid.: 42). In a first step, learners read the text individually. For their second and third reading, they take notes on the setting and characters depicted in the story. Similar to the stage directions in dramatic texts, they write down adjectives and adverbs which describe the characters and their (verbal) behaviour. They are also allowed to slightly adapt the mini-saga to transfer it entirely to a dramatic form. Dictionaries might be useful when learners frame their own text, which needs the concretisation of vague points within the mini-saga. In addition, the following questions may be helpful for learners to create their individual stage directions:

- What do you think the characters look like? What costumes and what make-up might they wear?
- What kind of facial expressions and gestures do you think they might use?
- What sort of voices do you think they have? How might a certain line be said (coldly, aggressively, with a sneer, in a loving voice, etc.)?
- How do you think the characters move around the stage? What props might they use?
- What is their relationship towards each other? How do they react physically to something another character might say?
- What do you think the setting looks like?

In order to contextualise and further specify the narration of the mini-saga, the following questions are valuable:

- What is special about the situation? What might have happened before? What could happen next?
- How do the characters feel? What do they think?

Another support, which takes up some time, however, is the composition of role biographies of the story's characters. This task prepares pupils for role-taking during the play. Every pupil chooses one character from the mini-saga and drafts a short biography for him/her using first-person narration. Similar to a résumé, the character introduces him-/herself in detail with reference to origin, social class, age, appearance, childhood, current situation, daily life, self-concept, state of mind and disposition. In doing so, learners are supposed to comply with the text and extract information about their character from it. At the same time, however, the features of the genre lead to the learners' having to invent details with regard to the characters' lives. These are only limited by their consistency with the overall conception of the character. As an aid for the composition of the role biographies, learners can use the following questions as guidance (cf. Nünning/Surkamp 2010: 192). Nevertheless, these questions should only serve as an orientation and should not be answered schematically, in a one-by-one fashion:

- **General questions:** What is your name? How old are you? What is your nationality?
- **Outward appearance:** How tall are you? What do your face and hair look like? How do you dress? How do you move? Is there anything significant about your facial expressions or gestures? What about your voice?
- **Childhood:** Where do you come from? Where did you grow up? Who were your parents? What did you like or dislike about them? Do you have any brothers or sisters? What do they mean to you? What type of experiences did you have at school? Was there any significant event in your childhood?
- **Everyday life and future prospects:** What is your profession? What does it mean to you? How would you describe your everyday life? What do you do in your spare time? Where would you like to live? What would you like to do in the future?
- **Self-image and relationship to other people:** What do you like or dislike about yourself? What do you fear? What are your dreams? How do you feel about your body? What do men mean to you? What do women mean to you?

Finally, learners perform the entire mini-saga. By experimenting with different kinds of articulation as well as with gestures, facial expressions and movements, learners can explore and try out how the characters behave, how they interact with and talk to each other (cf. Waldmann 2004: 118). In groups of advanced learners, pupils can also expand on the textual framework and improvise (or continue) the scene using their own words.

6 Cool Down and Reflections

After the scenic work with a mini-saga, it is important to offer the learners sufficient opportunities to digest the effects of the experience through appropriate cooling-down exercises. These exercises round off the process of acting and help to manage the transition to subsequent activities (see Wedel 2008, 2015). Secondly, taking time to reflect is crucial after every phase of acting. Learners should be able to talk about their experiences in their roles, their difficulties in acting out the text, the intentions they pursued in their acting, etc. The following questions might be useful in this context:

- What did we do and why? How did you feel? What did you want to express?

- How did the dramatic experience help you approach the text? Did it help you find your own interpretation?

Such reflection phases should be employed in order to make pupils realise that drama activities ought to be carried out seriously since they support them in finding an individual way of reading a story. Furthermore, learners experience that the preparatory exercises are not a dispensable 'playing around', but that they lead into the production and create an atmosphere which is conducive for the scenic work with narrative texts.

By contrasting different ways of staging a text, such reflection phases can also be used in the classroom to discuss various interpretations of one and the same mini-saga. Learners should have the opportunity to explain the choices they have made with regard to their enactments. They may inquire about the ideas and performances of the other groups. In this context, the following questions can be used as stimuli for discussions:

- What did you think about the performances? How did they differ from each other?
- How did the actors use body language and paralinguistic signs? What did gestures and/or facial expressions tell about a character's thoughts or feelings?
- How did the actors illustrate the characters' relationships? How did they interpret the situation?

7 Conclusion

Scenic explorations of mini-sagas encourage intensive reading and thorough textual work as well as in-depth engagement with the explicit and implicit content of the text. Pupils learn how to use non-verbal communication to convey meaning in conversations and they experience how much body language reveals about the thoughts and feelings of a person. All the drama-based methods presented above are highly transferable, that is they can easily be applied not only to other mini-sagas, but also to other short narrative and, of course, to dramatic texts.

Bibliography

Elis, Franziska (2015). Mit dramapädagogischen Methoden sprachliche und kommunikative Kompetenzen fördern. In: Hallet, Wolfgang/Surkamp, Carola (eds.). Handbuch Dramapädagogik und Dramendidaktik im Fremdsprachenunterricht. Trier: WVT, 89–115 .

Frommer, Harald (1995). Lesen und Inszenieren: Produktiver Umgang mit dem Drama auf der Sekundarstufe. Stuttgart: Klett.

Grieser-Kindel, Christin/Henseler, Roswitha/Möller, Stefan (2006). Method Guide. Schüleraktivierende Methoden für den Englischunterricht in den Klassen 5–10. Paderborn: Schöningh.

Maley, Alan/Duff, Alan (1982). Drama Techniques in Language Learning: A Resource Book of Communication Activities for Language Teachers. 2nd edition. Cambridge: Cambridge University Press.

Müller, Frank (1992). Dialog zwischen Text und Untertext: Theaterspielen als Sprechhandeln. Diskussion Deutsch 23:126, 365–374.

Nünning, Ansgar/Surkamp, Carola (2010). Englische Literatur unterrichten 1: Grundlagen und Methoden. 3rd edition. Seelze-Velber: Kallmeyer-Klett.

Proges, Wilfried (ed.) (2007a). Mini-Sagas: An Anthology of Fifty-Word Short Stories. Stuttgart: Reclam.

Proges, Wilfried (2007b). Nachwort. In: Proges, Wilfried (2007a), 165–183.

Scheller, Ingo (2004). Szenische Interpretation: Theorie und Praxis eines handlungs- und erfahrungsbezogenen Literaturunterrichts in Sekundarstufe I und II. Seelze-Velber: Kallmeyer.

Siebold, Jörg (1998). Zur Arbeit mit Mini-Sagas. Zielsprache Englisch 28:4, 17–24.

Siebold, Jörg (2015). Jedes Wort zählt! Und noch einmal Minisagas. Praxis Fremdsprachenunterricht Englisch 12:1, 4–8.

Surkamp, Carola (2014). Non-Verbal Communication: Why We Need It in Foreign Language Teaching and How We Can Foster It with Drama Activities. Scenario: Journal for Drama and Theatre in Foreign and Second Language Education VIII: 2, 28–43.

Surkamp, Carola/Elis, Franziska (2016). Dramapädagogik: Spielerisch Sprache lernen: Der Fremdsprachliche Unterricht Englisch 50: 142, 2–8.

Waldmann, Günter (2004). Produktiver Umgang mit dem Drama: Eine systematische Einführung in das produktive Verstehen traditioneller und moderner Dramenformen und das Schreiben in ihnen. Für Schule (Sekundarstufe I und II) und Hochschule. 4th edition. Baltmannsweiler: Schneider-Verlag Hohengehren.

Wedel, Heike (2008). Warming Up and Cooling Down. Zu einer vernachlässigten Dimension bei der Arbeit mit dramatischen Formen. In: Ahrens, Rüdiger/ Eisenmann, Maria/Merkl, Matthias (eds.). Moderne Dramendidaktik für den Englischunterricht. Heidelberg: Winter, 471–492.

Wedel, Heike (2015). Vor- und Nachbereitung von Theaterarbeit im Fremdsprachenunterricht. In: Hallet, Wolfgang/Surkamp, Carola (eds.). Handbuch Dramendidaktik und Dramapädagogik im Fremdsprachenunterricht. Trier: WVT, 307–318.

Petra Kirchhoff

Short – Shorter – #twitterfiction

1 Twitterfiction – a Literary Short Form in Social Networks

> Blaise Pascal didn't tweet and neither did Mark Twain. When it came to writing something short & sweet neither Blaise nor Mark had the time. (Simon Armitage)

Authors of Twitterfiction can use exactly 140 Unicode characters as well as auditive and audiovisual media to tell a story, continue one or just share their ideas with other users.[1] Twitter stories are published without a headline and are inevitably fragmentary. As Simon Armitage suggests in his quoted contribution to a Twitterfiction competition organized by the online journal of *The Guardian*, writing Twitterfiction is not as easy as it seems, but a rather time-consuming endeavour. Meanwhile, Twitterfiction has become known outside the Twitter-sphere (see overview of Twitter vocabulary in Figure 1). In 2012, 21 well-known authors followed *The Guardian's* call to send in Twitter fiction (see Appendix for all contributions). Anne Enright contributed the following piece of witty Twitterfiction:

> The internet ate my novel, but this is much more fun #careerchange #nolookingback oh but #worldsosilentnow Hey!

Her text ironically hints at the euphoria connected to the new literary medium. The tweeter imagines that the Internet has caused her novel to disappear (»the internet ate my novel«). Initial enthusiasm (»this is much more fun«) leads to a re-orientation of the speaker in the global communication network (#careerchange #nolookingback). However, this reorientation results in the perception of a void (»#worldsosilentnow«) and the author sends out a colloquial »Hey« into the extensive Twittersphere, calling for communication. In this text, the author cleverly uses the sign conventions of electronic communication, such as the hashtag (#), which is used to bundle the tweets of an estimated 320 million

---

1   At the moment Twitter is considering extending the 140-character limit and abandoning the chronological order of the tweets (cf. http://recode.net/2016/01/05/twitter-considering-10 000-character-limit-for-tweets/).

Twitter users according to thematic strands and to place individual tweets in
the discursive Twitter network.

To round up the competition, *The Guardian* asked its readers to choose one
140-character story out of the 21 contributions. The winner was Ian Rankin's
tweet. Here, Ian Rankin connects the new literary format to his work as a crime
writer:

> I opened the door to our flat and you were standing there, cleaver raised.
> Somehow you'd found out about the photos. My jaw hit the floor.

This example illustrates how a well-known genre like a crime novel or short
story is transformed into Twitterfiction. Aptly, the short piece focuses on what
might have been a turning point in a longer story. But it is not only pieces of
crime writing that are echoed in Twitterfiction. Neologisms such as *twillers*
(Twitter + thriller), *twaikus* (Twitter + Haiku) or *twistories* (Twitter + stories)
hint at more adaptations of other literary genres.

Twtrr	Original name of the project. »... we came across the word 'twitter', and it was just perfect. The definition was 'a short burst of inconsequential information,' and 'chirps from birds'. And that's exactly what the product was.« (Jack Dorsey, co-founder of Twitter)
Twitter	Micro-blogging, social networking service, which is mostly used on mobile devices. 320 million estimated users tweet worldwide 6000 tweets per second.
Tweet	A Twitter message, which is not allowed to exceed 140 signs.
	Logo of Twitter
#	Hashtag, formed from *hash* and *to tag*. With the #-sign, keywords can be highlighted in a Twitter message and used to group tweets according to topic.
To tweet	To send a tweet.
To retweet	To send a tweet again and thus include it in one's own timeline.
Follower	Twitter users can subscribe to other users' messages and thus become followers of the user. Their messages will then be shown in their own timeline.

Trending a topic	Concerted effort to draw the attention of many users to, for example, a cultural phenomenon (e.g. #GroundhogDay), a book publication (e.g. #potterheads: Harry Potter Fans) or to a celebrity (e.g. #beliebers: Justin Bieber Fans).
Timeline	List of subscribed messages in chronological order.
Twitterati	Enthusiastic users of the Twitter service.
Twittersphere	Collective of all tweets.

Fig. 1: Twitter vocabulary

Twitter fiction belongs to the so-called user-generated fiction on the Internet 2.0. Here, we are not just consumers of content, but we can also engage ourselves in active roles as writers, commentators or editors. Diverse content is made available to readers in real time, who in turn can share the content with other users of the Twittersphere. Even though the integration of images, audio and video material allows for paratextual extension, the (so far) strict textual format of a tweet also limits its genre-related possibilities. Acronyms and abbreviations are a natural fit for all kinds of social media usage, including Twitterfiction, which is in essence short and snappy communication. In order to tell a story and achieve poetic impact within the 140-character limit, many authors rely on abbreviations, especially for common phrases.

All tweets include specific structural features. These are highlighted in Ian Doescher's tweets from #TwitterFiction Festival 2015.[2] In his tweets, he entertainingly rewrites key scenes and dialogues from George Lucas' *Star Wars* in Shakespearean rhymed iambic pentameter.

---

2 The #TwitterFiction Festival goes back to 2014 when the Association of American Publishers and Penguin Random House joined efforts to promote the event. By the end of the festival, 50 authors from ten countries were showcased, and their tweets were seen by tens of millions of readers all over the globe (cf. http://twitterfictionfestival.com/about/).

Author`s full
name accord-
ing to his/her
twitter regis-
tration and
@username

Subscription as a *follower*
of a person

Time stamp

Functions: answer, retweet (number of retweets) and like-button

Fig. 2: Structure of a tweet

In a tweet, authors appear with their full name (Ian Doescher) as well as with
their username (@iandoescher). A Twitter account could also be used as a so-
called parody account, where living but also literary or historic personae supposedly send out tweets. Therefore, we see Edgar Allan Poe tweeting with the
username @Edgar_Allan_Poe. At the moment, 112,000 Twitter users follow
his Tweets on current events and enjoy reading excerpts from the work of the
seemingly resurrected American writer.

Fig. 3: Parody account of Edgar Allan Poe

As already shown with Ian Doescher's tweet, all tweets have a timestamp and
appear in chronological order. Readers can follow subsequent contributions
over a longer period of time by subscribing as a follower.

In Anna Todd's tweets, the protagonist Sloan has his say *(TwitterFiction Festival,* 2015). He describes himself as an average 16-year-old boy who finds the
mobile phone of his favourite actress and manages to gain access to her private
data. In the course of the story, Sloan considers possible actions and potential
consequences as he is tempted to make use of his newly gained power.

Fig. 4: Serial with 140-character tweets

From one tweet to the next, Anna Todd managed to win more and more fol-
lowers. Here, the chronological order of the tweets is essential for following
the storyline. Twitter's strict chronology opens up further opportunities for
authors. The clear structure allows not only one but several authors can use
different tweets to tell one and the same story from different perspectives. Nar-

rative events can thus be experienced in polyphonic narratives from different points of perception, as the following example with three contributing narrators illustrates.

Fig. 5: Multi-perspective Twitterfiction

In these tweets, three people witness a woman falling off the rooftop of a house. In minute intervals, their observations are released in the public Twittersphere. Interestingly, the narrative mode and the immediacy of communication convey a special sense of authenticity. It is now up to the reader to construct the story and to anticipate what might happen next. The reader might also speculate about the relationships between the narrators and the victim. As the story unfolds, the gaps and inconsistencies have to be perceived detective-like in order to piece together what »truly« happened.

Not only text can be used to tell a story. Authors are free to include images, sound and video recordings in the messages. Frankie Elliot uses pictures to develop her own literary voice. In a 'poetry to order' event, readers are asked to tweet key terms which the author then uses to develop short poems. The poems are written with an old-fashioned typewriter and shared with her readers by tweeting a picture of the literary product. With these 'Typewriter Poems',[3] the young author from Chicago took part in the #TwitterFiction Festival 2015.

---

3   Cf. http://frankielliottypewriter.tumblr.com. For more examples, go to http://www.ty-pewriterpoetry.com.

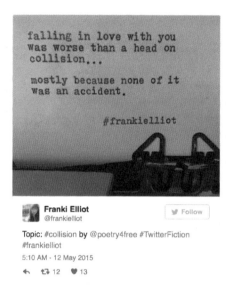

Fig. 6: Frankie Elliot's 'Typewriter Poems'

In this example (Figure 6), @frankielliot was sent the keyword #collision, marked with a hashtag, and developed an aphoristic comment on a fatal love encounter. In her work, image and text make an interesting blend. Bestselling author Celeste Ng also uses a mixture of photographs and text-tweets to tell a love story, but in the form of a literary scavenger hunt through a library (*TwitterFiction Festival*, 2015). In this story, the narrator pretends to have encountered hidden messages, which were used by two visitors to the library to communicate with each other (fig. 7).

Fig. 7: Celeste Ng's literary scavenger hunt

The first person narrator finds clues hidden under desks and library books and goes on to tell a story within a story. In this way, the author skilfully nests the turbulent love story inside the narrative frame of her library visit.

The literary examples in this paper only represent a limited number of ways to use Twitter creatively. Therefore, the following overview only highlights the most prominent literary Twitter formats.[4]

- A single story can be told with 140 characters. A literary role model for this short form is flash fiction: »For sale. Baby shoes, never worn«, ascribed to Ernest Hemingway.
- A continuing story can be tweeted in instalments by either one or several author/s.
- Twitter fiction can be told by a distinctly fictitious person. This person can either be purely fictional or the author can create a so-called parody account of a historic or living person, even if the latter is legally and ethically problematic.
- If answers to tweets or retweets are posted, a network of texts develops with the help of crowdsourcing.
- Pictures, videos, sounds and music can be tweeted alongside texts or instead of texts.

---

4   cf. Raguseo (2010) for other suggestions, e.g. about the dissemination of Twitterfiction.

As shown, Twitterfiction offers diverse communicative possibilities due to its brevity, the use of different media and a new symbolic language. The hashtag, for example, can be used to point to an already existing bundle of tweets about a certain topic, as well as to trigger a new conversation about a topic. On the one hand, the 140-character limit is a tough challenge to literary creativity. On the other, Twitterati can overcome temporal, local and medial boundaries with the use of the hashtag.

Some well-known writers like Ben Okri, author of »The Famished Road«, have taken to this new format. In an interview with »The Guardian« he describes his reasons for using Twitter in his creative work.

> Form follows adversity – we live in uncertain times. I think we need a new kind of writing that responds to the anxiety of our age and yet has brevity. My feeling is that these times are perfect for short, lucid forms. We need to get more across in fewer words. The Twitter poem tries to respond to this and the feeling of freedom (quoted in Flood 2009).

In Ben Okri's view, Twitter offers the opportunity to voice an immediate, artistic response to current issues and events. Therefore, he regularly publishes tweets at @benokri to share his poetry and his writing or to raise awereness of other writer's work.

2 Twitterfiction in the English Language Classroom

Reading or sharing texts via Facebook, WhatsApp, Twitter, SMS or MMS is part of most teenagers' everyday lives. Communication via social media is shown in recently published course book material. The fact that social media can be used to create exciting literary texts might be new information for most students, though.[5] In the language classroom, Twitterfiction can be used either receptively or productively. Sauers offers a number of interesting suggestions on how to make use of Twitterfiction in the language classroom (2009). Of course, considerations on data protection, privacy issues and a minimum age

---

5   Antenos-Conforti suggest potentially positive effects of the use of social media for lan-
     guage learning purposes. According to the authors of the same study, teachers also see
     great potential in using social media for meaningful interaction in foreign language
     learning (2009). Stevens analyses learner communication in a case study (2008). Dunlap
     and Lowenthal positively report on the use of Twitter to facilitate real-time communica-
     tion in courses at university level (Dunlap & Lowenthal, 2009).

for participation need to be taken seriously in a school context.[6] Therefore, it is important to state that some of the proposed activities could also be put into practice without students having to create their own Twitter accounts.

Reading and discussing Twitterfiction

First of all, students need to encounter examples of Twitterfiction. This new, sometimes enigmatic genre poses challenges to young readers: its brevity and the interplay of different media require careful reading and interpretation. On top of that, the sometimes complex communicational framework of Twitterfiction, e.g. in texts that have been sourced by a crowd of Twitterati, has to be given special attention. Questions like who sent the tweet or who retweeted a message, or how much time has passed between tweets, can help learners to work out genre-specific interpretations. Furthermore, they need a clear understanding of frequently used social media acronyms and abbreviations like the following:

Acronym or abbreviation	stands for ...
AMA	ask me anything
BFF	best friends forever
IDC	I don't care
IRL	in real life
JK	just kidding
LOL	laughing out loud
OMG	oh, my God
OMW	on my way
YOLO	you only live once

Fig. 8: Social media acronyms and abbreviations

Online quizzes on these short linguistic forms (e.g. on https://blog.bufferapp.com/social-media-acronyms-abbreviations) or quizzes made by students on the basis of charts can provide good teaching aids for introducing learners to this linguistic phenomenon in English. To follow up, learners could make up their own acronyms or abbreviations for phrases they perceive as relevant and fre-

---

6   In 2009, Twitter released new Terms of Service that omitted the requirement of 13 as a minimum age (https://twitter.com/tos for details). As a consequence, twitter does not ask the user's age when creating an account. The EU-initiative klicksafe.de offers further useful information.

quent in social media communication. As acronyms and abbreviations have become an integral part of oral and written communication, teaching these linguistic forms is worthwhile.

A good starting point for learners (at B2+-proficiency level in English) for reading is the online archive of past #Twitterfiction Festivals. On the website, they can explore and retrieve all of the Twitterfiction created in the past festival showcases. They can look up different genres or search for favourite authors. The contributions to »The Guardian Online« competition also make for excellent reading material (»The Guardian«, 2012; see Appendix). After going through a variety of texts, students can discuss, for instance, which of the texts they would like to translate into their mother tongue, or if they could think of a photograph to add to one of the texts (cf. worksheet 1).

#Twitterfiction: Questionnaire

Read through the tweets you are given. Then decide which ones you would choose in response to the questions.

1. If you had to translate one of the tweets, which one would you choose? Which of them would you find most difficult?
2. If you were asked to add a photograph or an illustration to one of them, which would it be?
3. If you had the chance of talking to one of the Twitterati, who would you choose?

Worksheet 1: #Twitterfiction: questionnaire

Very similar to working with poetry, students should be made aware of subtle nuances in expression and meaning. The choice of vocabulary in particular can add depth and a variety of potential interpretations to a very short text. A simple activity, in which learners have to decide the most powerful and poetic word in a certain context, can help them to notice and comprehend how language play in short texts works (cf. worksheet 2).

#Twitterfiction: Which word makes the best tweet?

Consider what makes a good piece of Twitterfiction. Read through the tweets and decide which of the words in bold works best.

@helenfielding
OK. Should not have logged on to your email but suggest if going on mar-riedaffair.com don't use our **neighbour's/children's/dog's** names as pass-word.

@harikunzru
I'm here w/ **disk/money**. Where ru? Mall too crowded to see. I don't feel safe. What do you mean you didn't send any text? Those aren't your guys?

@annieenright
The **dog/internet/mail** ate my novel, but this is much more fun #career-change #nolookingback oh but #worldsosilentnow Hey!

Worksheet 2: #Twitterfiction: Which word makes the best tweet?

In addition, the Twitterfiction generator on the #TwitterFiction Festival website provides a similar activity. Here, alternative suggestions for creating an interesting piece of Twitterfiction are presented (cf. http://twitterfictionfestival.com/instant/). The learners can click through the suggestions and decide in pairs or small groups which works best from their point of view.

In order to summarize all of the participants' findings, a list of rules and features of Twitterfiction needs to be worked out in groups for presentation to the whole class. This list can serve as a good basis for the next phase of creative language production.

Creative writing of Twitterfiction
Knowing the lexical and syntactic features, the communicational framework and the poetic qualities of Twitterfiction is a prerequisite for creative work with the genre. In several steps, students can learn how to write Twitterfiction themselves.

- Fragmentary tweets can be completed (e.g. on the website https://twitter.com/completedatweet).
- An important scene from classical texts (e.g. *Frankenstein, Dracula* or *Macbeth*) or texts from course books is selected and compacted to 140-character tweets.
- Keywords (e.g. #ocean, #Sundaynight) or common acronyms or abbreviations serve as a creative trigger for tweets, which could include audio or video material similar to @frankielliot's tweets on demand.
- A parody account serves as a creative basis for tweets and retweets.
- A story including multiple perspectives is crowdsourced in the class.

Once the features and rules of the genre are known, Twitterfiction already published can serve as input for writing longer texts like narrative descriptions, short stories, dialogues and plays. Learners can be asked to write a sequel or prequel to a tweet, which could serve as the first or last sentence of the new piece of writing.

On top of that, instances around Twitterfiction can be used to discuss ethical issues. In 2009, Flood reported that a Twitter user had pretended to be Maya Angelou and had continued to publish Twitterfiction and comments under her name.

> Last month it emerged that an imposter was on Twitter pretending to be the award-winning poet and memoirist Maya Angelou, with tweets including: »History, despite its wrenching pain / Cannot be unlived, and if faced / With courage, need not be lived again.« (Flood 2009)

At that time Maya Angelou was still alive. Immediately, ethical questions on the use of a parody account for living authors surface: Is it right to take on somebody else's name? Should Twitter change its terms of service in order to prevent impostors? In class, these questions can make for a lively discussion and contribute to learners' understanding of data and privacy protection in social media. Additionally, learners would have to research and use internet terminology and broaden their scope of up-to-date vocabulary.

It has been shown that teaching Twitterfiction in English classes is rewarding for many reasons. Learners encounter new linguistic forms like acronyms and abbreviations and poetic language in a new format that conveys immediacy and communicational authenticity. Additionally, Twitterfiction can serve as an excellent starting point for discussing ethical issues in the use of the social media.

Appendix
The Guardian Online: Twitter fiction 140-character novels
1. I know I said that if I lived to 100 I'd not regret what happened last night. But I woke up this morning and a century had passed. Sorry. (Geoff Dyer)
2. He said he was leaving her. »But I love you,« she said. »I know,« he said. »Thanks. It's what gave me the strength to love somebody else.« (James Meek)
3. She smiled, he smiled back, it was lust at first sight, but then she discovered he was married, too bad it couldn't go anywhere. (Jackie Collins)
4. I opened the door to our flat and you were standing there, cleaver raised. Somehow you'd found out about the photos. My jaw hit the floor. (Ian Rankin)

5. Blonde, GSOH, 28. Great! Ideal mate! Fix date. Tate. Nervous wait. She's late. Doh, just my fate. Wrong candidate. Blond – and I'm straight. (Blake Morrison)

6. »Your money or your life!« »I'm sorry, my dear, but you know it would kill me to lose my money," said the partially deaf miser to his wife. (David Lodge)

7. Sometimes we wonder why sorrow is so heavy when happiness is like helium. (AM Homes)

8. I had land, money. For each rejected novel I built one house. Ben had to drown because he bought Plot 15. My 15th book? The victim drowned. (Sophie Hannah)

9. Clyde stole a lychee and ate it in the shower. Then his brother took a bottle of pills believing character is just a luxury. God. The twins. (Andrew O'Hagan)

10. It's good that you're busy. Not great. Good, though. But the silence, that's hard. I don't know what it means: whether you're OK, if I'm OK. (Al Kennedy)

11. »It's a miracle he survived,« said the doctor. »It was God's will,« said Mrs Schicklgruber. »What will you call him?« »Adolf,« she replied. (Jeffrey Archer)

12. The internet ate my novel, but this is much more fun #careerchange #nolookingback oh but #worldsosilentnow Hey! (Anne Enright)

13. ur profile pic: happy – smiling & smoking. ur last post: »home!« ur hrt gave out @35. ur profile undeleted 6 months on. ur epitaph: »home!« (Patrick Neate)

14. I'm here w/ disk. Where ru? Mall too crowded to see. I don't feel safe. What do you mean you didn't send any text? Those aren't your guys? (Hari Kunzru)

15. She thanks me for the drink, but says we're not suited. I'm a little »intense«. So what? I followed her home. She hasn't seen anything yet. (SJ Watson)

16. OK. Should not have logged on to your email but suggest if going on marriedaffair.com don't use our children's names as password. (Helen Fielding)

17. Blaise Pascal didn't tweet and neither did Mark Twain. When it came to writing something short & sweet neither Blaise nor Mark had the time. (Simon Armitage)

18. Jack was sad in the orphanage til he befriended a talking rat who showed him a hoard of gold under the floor. Then the rat bit him & he died. (Charlie Higson)

19. Soften, my arse. I'm a geezer. I'm a rock-hard little bastard. Until I go mushy overnight for you, babe. #pears (India Knight)

20. Tom sent his wife's valentine to his mistress and vice versa. Poor Tom's a-cold and double dumped. (Jilly Cooper)
21. Rose went to Eve's house but she wasn't there. But Eve's father was. Alone. One thing led to another. He got 10 years. (Rachel Johnson)
(»Twitter fiction: 21 authors try their hand at 140-character novels,« 2012)

Bibliography

Antenos-Conforti, Enza (2009). Microblogging on Twitter: Social Networking in Intermediate Italian Classes. In: Lord, Gillian/Lomicka, Lara (eds.) The Next Generation Social Networking and Online Collaboration in Foreign Language Learning. CALICO, 59–90.

Dunlap, Joanna/Lowenthal, Patrick R. (2009). Tweeting the Night away: Using Twitter to Enhance Social Prestige. Journal of Information Systems Education, 20: 2, Special Issue, Impacts of the Web 2.0 and Virtual World Technologies in IS Education. http://patricklowenthal.com/publications/Using_Twitter_to_Enhance_Social_Presence.pdf. (12/02/2016)

Elliot, Frankie (2016). *franki ellliot. http://frankielliottypewriter.tumblr.com. (12/02/2016)

Flood, Alison (2009). Ben Okri releases new poem on Twitter. The Guardian Online. http://www.theguardian.com/books/2009/mar/25/ben-okri-poem-twitter. (12/02/2016)

Landeszentrale für Medien und Kommunikation (LMK) Rheinland-Pfalz (2016). Klicksafe.de. http://www.klicksafe.de. (12/02/2016)

Okri, Ben (2003). The Famished Road. London: Vintage.

Raguseo, Carla (2010). Twitter Fiction: Social Networking and Microfiction in 140 Characters. The Electronic Journal of Teaching English as a Second or Foreign Language, 13:4. http://www.tesl-ej.org/wordpress/issues/volume13/ej52/ej52int. (12/02/2016)

Sauers, Michael (2009). Twenty-five Interesting Ways to Use Twitter in the Classroom. http://www.slideshare.net/travelinlibrarian/twenty-five-interesting-ways-to-use-tw. (12/02/2016)

Stevens, Vance (2008). Trial by Twitter: The Rise and Slide of the Year's Most Viral Microblogging Plattform. TESL-EJ. Teaching English as a Second or Foreign Language. http://www.tesl-ej.org/ej45/int.html. (12/02/2016)

The Guardian. (2012). Twitter fiction: 21 authors try their hand at 140 character novels. http://www.theguardian.com/books/booksblog/2012/oct/15/twitter-fiction-your-stories. (12/02/2016)

Twitter. (2016). Allgemeine Geschäftsbedingungen von Twitter. https://twitter.com/tos. (12/02/2016)

Twitterfiction Festival (2015). http://twitterfictionfestival.com. (12/02/2016)

Typewriter Poetry (2016). http://www.typewriterpoetry.com. (12/02/2016)

Wagner, K. (2016). *Twitter Considering 10,000-Character Limit for Tweets.* http://
    recode.net/2016/01/05/twitter-considering-10 000-character-limit-for-
    tweets. (12/02/2016)

Senem Aydin

Short Stories and the Migration Experience

According to statistical information provided by UN Refugee Agency (2015), there are more than 60 million refugees in the world today. Due to human right abuses, poverty, social breakdown or particularly wars, many people are unable to receive any protection from their own states and hence require protection by other countries. The country where asylum seekers most frequently seek refugee status is Germany (UN Refugee Agency 2015). As a result, the themes of migration, refugees and asylum seekers have become extremely important not only in the media and political arena but also in schools, where school children experience this issue through meeting new children from different ethnic backgrounds and places. At a time when one in every 122 people in the world has been forced to flee persecution, violence or war (UN Refugee Agency 2015), it is appropriate for children to be sensitized about these issues, which are linked to concepts such as justice, equality, tolerance and freedom.

In their foreign language curricula, all German federal states aim to enhance tolerance and respect by students towards people from other cultural and ethnic backgrounds. However, although school children can observe a rapid increase of mobility in their surroundings and experience a similar sense of displacement as a result, for example, of moving from one city to another or stay abroad for a long period, it is difficult to expect children to understand the experiences of refugees without access to intercultural learning by means of carefully selected teaching materials.

> Focusing foremostly on intercultural learning in language teaching, the language classroom can and should study multicultural and refugee stories because an intercultural speaker finds interacting with people from other cultures with their distinctive perspectives enriching. For the older age group of young learners, I suggest multicultural picturebooks can be used to develop communicative competence, language awareness and learning strategies, literary competence, intercultural competence, media, visual and critical literacy and an awareness of global issues (Bland 2013: 32).

Within the theme of migration, there has been a noteworthy growth in children's literature dealing with the issue of seeking asylum in a foreign country (Hope 2008: 298). Short stories in picturebooks provide teachers and learners with an opportunity to explore this complex issue in an age-appropriate manner.

It is hard to define a short story; however, Werlich (1999) explains its main characteristics as being centered around one incident, organizing character and action into a simple plot, focusing on a single turning-point, a short period of time, one setting and a limited number of characters. Hope (2008: 232) claims that these kinds of stories play an important role in showing that refugee children are ordinary children in extraordinary circumstances.

Stories in picturebooks have been used in English language teaching for over four decades (Mourao 2015: 199). Alongside their established curricular importance, short stories have proven to be suitable teaching materials to boost cultural openness to linguistic and cultural diversity as well as to teach children simple yet valuable lessons about life (Thaler 2008: 96).

1 The Potential of Picturebooks in the EFL Classroom

The short stories in picturebooks have great potential to foster imagination, creativity, openness and critical thinking. It is widely recognized that engagement with stories contributes to learners' linguistic, literary, affective and intercultural development.

1.1 Linguistic Development

New words and phrases can be introduced and revised by using stories since they contain diverse, memorable language that supports linguistic development. Pictures in stories help learners to deduce the meaning of unknown words from an authentic context that provides a basis for »coping with language intended for native speakers« (Collie/Slater 2001: 4). Such authentic input supports linguistic acquisition, while pictures enable learners to make use of visual clues to grasp the context. As this gives students an opportunity to develop their existing L1 learning strategies, the foreign language teacher should consider the learners' L1 knowledge and build on it. In addition, Lazar (1993: 23) argues that learners' aesthetic development can be boosted through teaching literature because they can realize how the language used in literary texts differs from daily language.

Since the main goal of foreign language teaching to young learners is developing oral skills and communicative competence, the main focus is on creating a repertoire of basic vocabulary and formulaic expressions to be used in different conversational situations. However, development of communicative competence entails more than merely articulating ritualized sentences or memorized chunks; rather, students should be provided with opportunities to use language spontaneously (Thornbury 2005: 13). Stories allow them to experiment with the target language by learning other linguistic elements than prefabricated utterances (Edelenbos et al. 2006: 9). In this regard, using authentic stories and encouraging learners to understand and learn new words can give them a strong sense of success in learning with a 'real' book.

Finally, it should be kept in mind that the linguistic competence of young learners is not as developed as their cognitive and affective competences, which might cause some challenges in using stories. That is, although their knowledge of the world and language learning experiences from their L1 are more advanced, their L2 linguistic level is not yet sufficient to understand certain texts (Bland 2013: 35). However, picturebook stories allow learners to decode even demanding texts since visual images help to communicate word meanings in »extremely minimalist ways« (Enever 2006: 61). Therefore, the teacher should focus more strongly on the illustrations than the text so that learners can decode the pictures and thereby learn to think in a creative way.

1.2 Literary Development

While reading and listening, especially young learners encounter for the first time basic literary elements, such as plot, setting, characters and stylistic devices. They can then integrate their previous experience and personal knowledge into interpreting stories in an individual way, making use of predicting, intelligent guessing and hypothesizing to develop their personal interpretation (Legutke et al. 2009: 73). Therefore, stories lay the foundations of literary competence in the target language. Moreover, they develop critical thinking abilities by means of reading or listening to a text in a reflective manner, which may foster a deeper insight into social issues, such as human relations, inequality or power, as Dolan explains:

> Early childhood educators who facilitate the development of critical literacy encourage children to interrogate societal issues such as poverty, education, equity, and equality and institutions such as family and school in order to critique the structures that serve as norms as well as to demonstrate how these norms are not experienced by all members of society. Critical literacy is not merely about educating children about critical ways of seeing and questioning (Dolan 2012:5).

Greene (1995: 5) claims that children's literature, especially picturebooks, provide limitless opportunities for teaching critical literacy, encouraging »social imagination« and incorporating global perspectives in foreign language teaching.

1.3 Affective Development

Listening to stories in class is a common social experience. Sharing laughter, sadness, excitement and disappointment can support the emotional development of students. Also stories about migration and refugee issues in authentic picturebooks offer a multitude of possibilities for fostering affective development since they dwell upon a variety of universal feelings like fear, grief and confusion (Dolan 2014: 95). Therefore, they are quite suitable for exploring topics like empathy, tolerance and justice. Although they are suitable for providing a framework for exploring these topics, a further crucial factor for the effective implementation of stories is a well-planned scaffolding process based on carefully chosen teaching goals.

> It is very important that all learners are helped to achieve affective responses to the materials they use, for without affective engagement there is no chance of effective and durable acquisition. This involves learners responding with their emotions – by, for example, laughing, getting excited, feeling happy, feeling sympathy, feeling affection (Tomlinson 2015: 284).

By humanizing English language teaching, stories have the potential to foster moral reasoning skills, emotional intelligence and empathy. The teacher should take both students' cognitive and affective levels into account while setting teaching goals, creating a supportive learning environment, and designing activities and materials to build up confidence and pleasure in using picturebooks (Arnold/Brown 1999: 1–3).

1.4 Intercultural Development

Storybooks reflect the culture of the characters involved and include information on cultural aspects, which enriches intercultural understanding. Carefully selected storybooks provide a very rich resource for raising awareness of diversity, developing positive attitudes towards other cultures and building empathy for others (Ellis/Brewster 2014: 8). The teacher should therefore choose stories which arouse curiosity and willingness to learn more about the target culture:

> The role of the teacher is to encourage and to help bring about discovery, drawing attention to the fact that the differences in relation to the pupils' own habits and day-to-day lives are to be seen in a positive light as they add to, by definition, the sum of the pupils' knowledge of humanity and of the world (Brewster, Ellis, Girard 1992: 32).

To achieve this goal, stories can be used to take learners on educational journeys to view other cultures from different angles in order to reveal the similarities and differences between these cultures. In this way, critical thinking is nurtured by discussing global issues like human rights, global civic responsibility, which constitute the notion of Delanoy's intercultural competence (Delanoy 2006: 240). By focusing on children's emotions due to linguistic and cultural difficulties in critical situations, picture storybooks in particular provide a rich resource for developing critical cultural awareness since learners put themselves into the shoes of characters in the story. In doing so, students are prepared for living in an increasingly diverse society and they learn to recognize and respect the normality of diversity in all areas of human life.

2 Criteria for Selecting Stories

Although many picturebooks are available for treating social topics like migration, the majority of foreign language teachers do not feel confident to integrate such up-to-date literature into their teaching, being instead generally inclined to rely on a limited repertoire of children's books.

The large number of picturebooks about migration and refugee issues, some of which are listed in the conclusion to this article, raises the question of the criteria for selecting appropriate stories. Alongside learners' cognitive, linguistic and affective abilities, teaching goals and conditions play a crucial role in choosing a story for a given teaching context. Dolan (2014: 100–102) divides these criteria into seven categories while choosing a picturebook about migration and refugee issues. She asks the following questions:

> **Cover:** What do you notice on the cover of the picturebook? What are the most important features on the cover? What is the title of the book? What does this title mean to you? Has the book won any awards? Are they displayed on the cover? What colors dominate the cover design? What is in the foreground? What is in the background? What is the significance of the placement? Are there any visual images in the background to consider? What refugee clues (if any) are provided on the cover?
>
> **Representation of asylum seekers and refugees:** Are asylum seekers and/or refugees represented on the cover? How are they portrayed? Is the main character looking at you? How does this affect you? If the character is looking at you, what might he/she be demanding from you? Is the character looking away or at someone or something else? How does this affect you?

Setting: What setting is portrayed on the cover and in other illustrations? Describe the setting in geographical terms, e.g. find its location on a map. When do you think this story is taking place? What visual and textual clues are provided on the cover, jacket, and within the author's note? How is the setting important in the context of this picturebook about refugees? How are colour, texture, and motif used to represent the setting of the story?

Illustration style: Are the illustrations realistic, folk art, surreal or impressionistic? How might the style of illustration add to the mood or theme of the book? How does the style contribute to the understanding of a refugee's experience?

End pages: What do you notice about the end pages? Do they contain a visual narrative? Do they contribute to the visual continuity of the picturebook? Do they represent the story of refugees in any way?

Book jacket (where book jackets are included): What information is contained in the front and back book jacket? How does the jacket information (if any) help to establish historical background information for the story? How does this information help you to understand the story? What clues are given about the historical facts (if any) and fictional aspects being presented?

Title page: What information is included on the title page? Is a visual image included on the title page? Is the image within the story? If so, what is the significance? If the image is not within the story, what symbolic meaning does it hold?

Keeping this useful list of criteria in mind, a picturebook treating the refugee experience from a primary school child's perspective called »Azzi in Between« was chosen to sensitize young learners of English as a foreign language to this issue. The book was written by Sarah Garland in 2012 and contains 36 pages. It is a fictional story based on the author's personal experiences of working with refugees in New Zealand. The book, which is recommended by Amnesty International in the UK, tells the story of a family that has to escape from a country in the Middle East due to war. Azzi and her family have to leave their vivid lives to survive; however, her grandmother, whom Azzi desperately misses, has to stay behind in the homeland. After a frightening journey, they reach their new destination in the UK, where the perplexing newness of everything from language and food to school makes Azzi afraid.

This sensitive story is entirely presented in a graphic format with simple sentences under each panel providing clear illustrations, which stimulate imagination and interpretative skills. The color selection to depict certain situations is well-planned, e.g. war is shown in shades of grey, which contrast with the bright colors in Azzi's home life.

Unfortunately, there is an unjustified belief that picturebooks are suitable solely for young learners; however, it can be maintained that they are also appropriate for raising sensitive issues with learners at older ages since they offer realistic contexts for moving beyond the typical thematic language of English classes to treat more thought-provoking topics (Dolan 2014: 127). While »Azzi in Between« is suitable for young learners from fourth grade on, owing to its global message about the difficult experiences of a refugee family, it is also quite informative for adult learners.

In order to fully exploit stories to enhance intercultural learning, choosing appropriate stories is not enough since they do not work on their own. Another challenge for foreign language teachers to meet is finding the appropriate methodology, i.e. planning a well-structured teaching sequence with meaningful activities to profit as much as possible from the stories for intercultural enrichment.

3 Storytelling Suggestions for »Azzi in Between«

By designing cognitively demanding and linguistically manageable activities, the teacher should make learning with stories a motivating experience for the learners. However, this is not an easy task if the stories are applied to teach delicate and complex migration issues:

> Evidence is very limited about how teachers develop learners' curiosity and openness, and which types of activities and tasks are most effective for children of different ages in helping them develop skills to 'step into another's shoes' or understand the complexity of intercultural interaction (Driscoll/ Simpson 2015: 175).

According to Volkmann (2015: 256), it is important to select activities that »present texts as catalysts for intercultural and transcultural understanding and exchange«. In the following sections, pre-, while- and post-storytelling phases will be explained, briefly accompanied by some practical implications for teaching »Azzi in Between« to provide suitable scaffolding. The focus will not be on well-known storytelling strategies, e.g. pre-teaching unknown key vocabulary, but on more specific ideas.

3.1 Pre-storytelling Phase

Activities in the pre-storytelling phase aim at a basic understanding of the story to help students meet the learning goals and experience the story session as an enjoyable process. This involves teaching or reviewing key words, raising students' awareness of essential grammatical patterns, presenting useful expressions for active student involvement in discussions, and activating their previous experience and world knowledge to lead them into the topic. Other possibilities at this stage include motivating activities to arouse curiosity and create expectations concerning the story's main characters and plot. The following teaching ideas for the pre-storytelling phase of »Azzi in Between« exemplify this stage.

The teacher can make use of different sound effects to raise student curiosity in the topic. There are many stimulus sound libraries on the internet, e.g. BBC School Radio. The teacher may ask his/her students to write down or mention their feelings about the voices in a recording called »heartstorming« since it is feelings rather than ideas that are discussed. Afterwards, the teacher can ask the students about recent developments in current global affairs.

Since students are probably exposed to such issues in their daily lives, they can be asked to share their own knowledge and experiences about refugees: Where do they come from? Why do they come? The teacher can use a map for these questions. If the learners' L2 level is insufficient to discuss the issue, a brief discussion may take place in L1.

In a previous lesson, the teacher could have asked the students to bring along an object from home that symbolizes »home« for each student. In the lead-in phase, volunteers can present their objects and explain why this specific object is representative of their homeland or home town. Alternatively, they can create and display in class picture or object collages concerning the given topic. Students can also be asked what food they associate with their home or what food they miss most when they are away from home. In discussing this, students can be encouraged to give details about ingredients, smells, colors and tastes.

Additionally, the teacher can read out a few pages from the story and ask the students to imagine and draw the main character. This might be quite interesting for »Azzi in Between« since it is usually difficult to guess whether Azzi is a male or female name. Alternatively, the teacher can show the book cover depicting a little girl holding her teddy bear as she walks through a war-torn landscape: Look at the cover of the book. What do you see? What do you think the book is about? How do you think the character feels? Some illustrations from the story can also be enlarged as picture flashcards. Students can be asked to predict the correct sequence of the events.

Finally, the teacher can dictate two pictures that contain important details of the story, and make the students draw the pictures, e.g. illustrations of Azzi's old and new house. The students' drawings can then be compared after the story has been read.

3.2 While-storytelling Phase

The while-storytelling phase should include at least two readings. The first reading is for general comprehension (reading for the gist of the text), whereas the second or, in some cases, the third reading is used to have students concentrate on specific details. The first time, it is more appropriate to read fluently without stopping too often to ask for comments. During the second reading, there can be pauses for questions or repetitions. This phase should include original activities to keep curiosity and tension high.

During the first reading, the teacher can play background music suitable for the topic. This activates learners' multisensory learning channels and helps them enter the mood of the story. The teacher may interrupt at one or two places to ask learners to predict what will happen in the story.

During the second reading, the teacher can darken the classroom by drawing the curtains. Depending on their age group, students may be sitting in a circle on the floor or in their chairs facing a wall on which the teacher has already fixed a mixture of large flashcards containing illustrations from the book as well as plot-related pictures from magazines. The teacher can then shine a torch light on the relevant picture while students listen to the story again.

Another creative while-reading activity for better learner involvement is making students create sound effects alongside the teacher's second reading. »Azzi in Between« is quite suitable for this technique when particular images are presented, as in the following examples:

Page 1 / Student 1: sounds of bombs, combat planes. (Garland: Azzi in Between (2012)

Sometimes they looked over the garden wall at the soldiers marching by.

Page 3, Student 2: sounds of marching soldiers, e.g. footsteps by tapping on the table
(Garland: Azzi in Between (2012).

Students can also be given different illustrations from the book and asked to put
the pictures into the right order on the blackboard while the teacher reads the
story out for a second time. There are 130 illustrations or panels in this story
book, from which a manageable number can be chosen depending on the size
of the class.

Since the events in the story follow a particular sequence, from fleeing the
homeland to arriving in the UK and starting a new school, the teacher can ask
students to fill in a timeline while listening to the story for a second time. Another activity is to give students small word cards containing certain keywords
from the story. Students then number them according to their order of appearance in the story.

Finally, it should be remembered that while-storytelling activities should be
plausible and create a smooth, meaningful transition to the post-storytelling
phase.

3.3 Post-storytelling Phase

Müller-Hartman/Schocker-von Ditfurth (2004: 82) explain the aim of this stage
as the »consolidation of the language« and the »extension of content«. Learners
should be given enough time to practice or improve linguistic elements, such as
newly-learned vocabulary items or simple grammar structures via constructive
activities. Moreover, reconstructive and creative activities should be used to
encourage more empathy with the content and foster imagination (Cameron
2001: 176).

The first goal of activities in this phase is checking comprehension. As an
alternative to typical comprehension activities, such as true/false questions,

summaries, gap-filling exercises or wh-questions, the teacher can try out more enjoyable and stimulating tasks after the story has been read.

First, instead of a student, the teacher may be hot-seated so that the students can ask the teacher questions about the story. Alternatively, the teacher can show illustrations of key events from the story for students to summarize from memory. The same activity can also be implemented using picture dice. In this case, pupils get into groups of four, with each group receiving two dice on which different illustrations from the story have been fixed. Group members throw the dice and describe what they can remember about the scene on top to the rest of the group. Once all the illustrations have been explained, two groups get together to replay the game with four dice with new illustrations. This activity reinforces story comprehension by recapping it in an enjoyable way. Students can then work together to summarize the main message of the story through creative posters depicting the central scenes of the story.

At this stage, a role play of certain dialogues from the story can be used to make students actively use newly-learned vocabulary items and build empathy by getting into the shoes of the characters. Real objects and costumes can be provided, e.g. a teddy bear for Azzi. This activity can be combined with a class survey conducted by the students asking questions like »Imagine you are living in a country where war has been declared. Bombs are falling. You have one minute to prepare your luggage and leave your home. What will you take with you? Why?« Alternatively, students can write a postcard or letter to Azzi to understand her situation better.

Since this story is somewhat open-ended, the students can be invited to create a complementary page to the picturebook on which they demonstrate via illustrations and speech bubbles what Azzi and her family will be doing five years later. To extend these stories, the teacher can encourage students to use a creative app or webpage for designing online picturebooks, e.g. www.littlebirdtales.com, Buncee for Edu, Book Writer One.

In »Azzi in Between«, the way the refugee family plants beans from their former home in the school garden, provides a powerful metaphorical image of gaining new roots, before growing and bearing fruit on a new soil, as her grandmother says at the end of the story: »New beans, new life.« Some dedicated teachers could enrich their repertoire of creative activities by combining the storytelling experience with a cross-curricular activity like growing beans in the classroom. Each student can join the experiment of planting beans and waiting for them to grow. The teacher can also organize a visit to a refugee camp or invite a group of refugee children to the classroom to enable the students to gain a deeper understanding of the challenges of starting a new life.

4 Conclusion

This article has discussed the potential of stories in picturebooks to depict the refugee experience and raise the awareness of students about experiences like persecution, flight and migration. Such stories can serve as a suitable vehicle to sensitize non-refugee or indigenous readers to their refugee classmates or peers who have arrived in a new country. However, as Dolan warns, it is important that stories are well-written and realistic:

> Simply increasing students' access to multicultural literature is not sufficient in itself as a strategy for engaging with global and justice perspectives. In many situations, educators struggle with development concepts and do not move beyond superficial descriptions of lifestyles in exotic places. In some cases, reading more about the world can negatively influence the development of intercultural understanding as negative stereotypes are reinforced. Hence, it is important for educators to choose books with maximum potential for exploring global and justice perspectives (Dolan 2014: 108).

A selected list of recommended picturebooks is presented below to help foreign language teachers choose suitable stories depending on the specific learner profile and teaching goals:

> How Many Days to America? A Thanksgiving Story (1990); Dreaming of America: An Ellis Island Story (2000); My Dog (2001); Mary Hoffman's The Colour of Home (2002); A Picnic in October (2004); Persepolis (2004); My Name was Hussein (2004); The Roses in My Carpets (2004); The Lost Boys of Sudan (2005); Tree Girl (2005); Ziba Came on a Boat (2007); The Arrival (2007); The Island (2007); Four Feet, Two Sandals (2007); Grandfather's Journey (2008); Muktar and the Camels (2009); Gervelie's Journey: A Refugee Diary (2009); So Far from the Sea (2009); My Name is Sangoel (2009); The Silence Seeker (2009); Mali Under the Night Sky, A Lao Story of Home (2010); The Happiest Refugee: A Memoir (2011); The Little Refugee (2011).

Due to a rapid increase in international mobility and a fast-changing, multicultural world, the concept of »global education« has gained more significance in that pupils' horizons need to be broadened about global topics like human rights and environmental issues (Özkul 2012: 17). To become interculturally competent, one must gain the ability to behave appropriately in intercultural situations and to retain a stable self-identity while mediating between cultures (Jensen 1995: 41). For this purpose, students should be motivated to understand first their own identity, inner world and self, then people in their surrounding:

Without stories, and without an understanding of stories, we don't understand ourselves, we don't understand the world about us. And we don't understand the relations between ourselves and those people around us. Because what stories give us is an insight into ourselves, a huge insight into other people, other cultures, other places (Morpurgo 2014).

Although many refugee stories in children's literature are available which offer an educationally ideal context to share the thoughts and emotions experienced by migrants with learners, still a restricted set of books tend to be used for teaching literature within English language teaching. Teachers should bear in mind that stories are a powerful pedagogic medium, especially at an early age, for training students' minds to reflect about difficult situations and imagine ways of solving problems.

Bibliography

Arnold, Jane/Brown, Douglas (1999). A Map of the Terrain. In: Arnold, Jane (ed.). Affect in Language Learning. Cambridge: CUP, 1–24.

BBC School Radio. www.bbc.co.uk/learning/schoolradio/subjects/earlylearning/stimulussoundslibrary. (27/12/2015)

Bland, Janice (2013). Children's Literature and Learner Empowerment. Children and Teenagers in English Language Education. London: Bloomsbury.

Brewster, Jean/Ellis, Gail/Girard, Denis (1992). The Primary English Teacher's Guide. Harmondsworth: Penguin.

Bunting, Eve/Carpenter, Nancy (2004). A Picnic in October. New York: Houghton Mifflin Harcourt.

Bunting, Eve/Peck, Beth (1990). How Many Days to America? A Thanksgiving Story. New York: Clarion Books.

Bunting, Eve (2009). So Far from the Sea. New York: Houghton Mifflin Harcourt.

Bunting, Eve/Stahl, Ben F. (2000). Dreaming of America: An Ellis Island Story. USA: Troll Bridge Water Books.

Cameron, Lynne (2001). Teaching Languages to Young Learners. Cambridge: CUP.

Collie, Joanne/Slater, Stephen (2007). Literature in the Language Classroom: A Resource Book of Ideas and Activities. Cambridge: CUP.

Delanoy, Werner (2006). Transculturality and (Inter)-Cultural Learning in the EFL-Classroom. In: Delanoy, Werner/Volkmann, Laurenz (eds.). Cultural Studies in the EFL-Classroom. Heidelberg: Winter, 233–248.

Do, Anh (2011). The Happiest Refugee: A Memoir. Sydney: Allen & Unwin.

Do, Anh (2011). The Little Refugee. Sydney: Allen & Unwin.

Dolan, Anne M. (2012). The Potential of Picture Story Books for Teaching Migration, in Proceedings of 33rd iBbY International Congress. Crossing Boundaries: Translations and Migrations, 1–18. http://www.ibby.org.uk/congress2012. (20/12/2015)

Dolan, Anne M. (2014). Intercultural Education, Picturebooks and Refugees: Approaches for Language Teachers. CLELEjournal 2:1, 92–109.

Dolan, Anne M. (2014). Making Development Issues Accessible through Picturebooks. In: Waldron, Fionnuala (ed.). Proceedings of the Irish Association for Social, Scientific and Environmental Education. Annual Conference 2013, 124–144. https://www.spd.dcu.ie/site/education/staff_details/documents/MeetingtheChallengesofaGlobalisedWorld.pdf. (25/12/2015)

Driscoll, Patricia/Simpson, Helen (2015). Developing Intercultural Understanding in Primary Schools. In: Bland, Janice (ed.). Teaching English to Young Learners: Critical Issues in Language Teaching with 3–12 Year Olds. London: Bloomsbury, 167–180.

Edelenbos, Peter/Johnstone, Richard/Kubanek, Angelika (2006). The Main Pedagogical Principles Underlying the Teaching of Languages to Very Young Learners. Languages for the Children of Europe: Published Research. Good Practice & Main Principles. European Commission.

Ellis, Gail/Brewster, Jean (2014). Tell it again! The Storytelling Handbook for Primary English Language Teachers. British Council.

Enever, Janet (2006). The Use of Authentic Picture Books in the Development of Critical Visual and Written Literacy in English as a Foreign Language. In: Enever, Janet/Schmidt-Schönbein, Gisela (eds.). Picture Books and Young Learners of English. Berlin: Langenscheidt, 59–70.

Garland, Sandra (2012). Azzi in Between. London: Frances Lincoln.

Graber, Janet/Mack, Scott (2009). Muktar and the Camels. New York: Henry Holt and Company (BYR).

Greder, Armin (2007). The Island. Sydney: Allen & Unwin.

Greene, Maxine (1995). Releasing the Imagination: Essays on Education, the Arts and Social Change. San Francisco: Jossey Bass.

Heffernan, John/McLean, Andrew (2001). My Dog. Australia: A Margaret Hamilton book from Scholastic Australia.

Hoffman, Mary (2003). The Colour of Home. London: Frances Lincoln.

Hope, Julia (2008). One Day We Had to Run: The Development of the Refugee Identity in Children's Literature and its Function in Education. Children's Literature in Education 39:4, 295–304.

Jensen, Annie A. (1995). Defining Intercultural Competence – A Discussion of its Essential Components and Prerequisites. In: Sercu, Lies (ed.). Intercultural

Competence – A New Challenge for Language Teachers and Trainers in Europe. Aalborg: Aalborg University Press, 41–52.

Kyuchukov, Hristo. (2004). My Name was Hussein. Pennsylvania: Boyds Mills Press.

Landowne, Youme (2010). Mali under the Night Sky: A Lao Story of Home. United States: Cinco Puntos Press.

Lazar, Gillian (1993). Literature and Language Teaching. Cambridge: CUP.

Legutke, Michael/Müller-Hartmann, Andreas/Schocker-von Ditfurth, Marita (2009). Teaching English in the Primary School. Stuttgart: Schöningh.

Lofthouse, Liz (2007). Ziba Came on a Boat. San Diego/CA: Kane Miller Books.

Marjane, Satrapi (2004). Perpapolis. New York: Pantheon.

Morley, Ben (2009). The Silence Seeker. London: Tamarind Publishers.

Morpurgo, Michael (2014). http://www.storymuseum.org.uk/about-us/testimonials/. (22/12/2015)

Mourao, Sandie (2015). The Potential of Picturebooks with Young Leaners. In: Bland, Janice (ed.). Teaching English to Young Learners: Critical Issues in Language Teaching with 3–12 Year Olds. London: Bloomsbury, 199–217.

Müller-Hartmann, Andreas/Schocker-von Ditfurth, Marita (2004). Introduction to English Language Teaching. Stuttgart: Klett.

Özkul, Senem (2012). Speaking Foreign Body Language: Fostering Intercultural Nonverbal Competence in ELT Classrooms. Praxis Fremdsprachenunterricht 05:12, 16–17.

Robinson, Anthny/Young, Annemarie (2009). Gervelie's Journey: A Refugee Diary. London: Frances Lincoln Children's Books.

Say, Allen (2008). Grandfather's Journey. Boston: Houghton Mifflin Harcourt.

Shea, Pegi (1995). The Whispering Cloth: a Refugee's Story. Honesdale/PA: Boyds Mills.

Tan, Shaun (2000). The Lost Thing. Australia/New Zealand: Lothian Books.

Tan, Shaun (2007). The Arrival. Arthur A. Levine Books.

Thaler, Engelbert (2008). Teaching English Literature. Paderborn: UTB.

Thornbury, Scott (2005). Awareness, Appropriation and Autonomy. English Language Teaching Professional, 40, 11–13.

Tomlinson, Brian (2015). Developing Principled Materials for Young Learners of English as a Foreign Language. In: Bland, Janice (ed.). Teaching English to Young Learners: Critical Issues in Language Teaching with 3–12 Year Olds. London: Bloomsbury, 279–293.

UN Refugee Agency (2015). https://www.uno-fluechtlingshilfe.de/fluechtlinge/zahlen-fakten.html. (23/12/2015)

Volkmann, Laurenz (2015). Opportunities and Challenges for Transcultural Learning and Global Education via Literature. In: Bland, Janice (ed.).

Teaching English to Young Learners: Critical Issues in Language Teaching with 3–12 Year Olds. London: Bloomsburry, 237–262.

Werlich, Egon (1999). The Learner's Vocabulary for Text Analysis. Berlin: Cornelsen.

Williams, Karen/Mohammed, Khadra (2007). Four Feet, Two Sandals. Grand Rapids: Eerdmans Books for Young Readers.

Williams, Karen/Mohammed, Khadra (2009). My Name Is Sangoel. Grand Rapids/Michigan: Eerdmans Books for Young Readers.

Williams, Mary (2005). Brothers in Hope: The Story of the Lost Boys of Sudan. New York: Lee & Low Books.

Stephanie Schaidt

That's so Meta

Metafictive Picturebooks in the EFL Classroom

In the last few years, a growing number of picturebooks with metafictive devices has been published. According to Lewis (2001: 94), such devices »are essential to the postmodernist enterprise, with its sustained attack on all manifestations of authoritative order and unity.«[1] Metafictive picturebooks constantly transgress boundaries and play with literary conventions. It is exactly this unconventionality and playfulness which makes them such a rich resource for the EFL classroom.

1 What is Metafiction?

Metafiction refers to »fictional writing which self-consciously and systematically draws attention to its status as an artefact in order to pose questions about the relationship between fiction and reality« (Waugh, 1984: 2). It draws the readers' attention to the nature of literary texts. Through the use of a number of metafictive strategies, writers play with literary and cultural conventions and traditions and so point to the status of the text as a text. In the case of picturebooks, these metafictive strategies can be applied to both the verbal and the visual text. In this article, however, the focus will be put on the verbal text.

2 Metafictive Strategies in Picturebooks

In the following, a number of metafictive strategies will be presented, drawing on examples of self-referential picturebooks. The books chosen do not always make use of all the strategies discussed, but in most cases there is more than one strategy employed in the text.

---

1 Lewis (2001: 100), however, further remarks that metafiction should not be equated with postmodernism. Whereas postmodernism is historical, metafictive devices have been used by different writers »at many periods throughout history.«

2.1 Book-within-a-Book Structure

Some picturebooks are metafictive to the extent that they make use of a book-within-a-book or story-within-a-story structure (*mis en abyme*). The Jacket (Hall 2014), for example, tells the story of Book who feels very lonely because no child appreciates him until he is discovered by a little girl who reads him and loves him. When the girl's dog splashes mud on Book, the girl is very sad but then solves the problem by creating a yellow book jacket with two eyeholes for Book. This book jacket looks exactly like the jacket of the book the reader is holding. Therefore, this very book seems to be actually part of the story.

Also in Emily Gravett's *Wolves* (2005), the book the reader reads is embedded in the narrative: Rabbit borrows a book from the library which is entitled »Wolves« and written by Emily Grrrabbit. While Rabbit is reading the book, the reader reads along. In both cases, the book-within-a-book structure highlights the fact that a narrative can never quite reach the base of reality because it refers in a frame-within-a-frame way to other narratives. This might draw the readers' attention to the fact that narrative worlds are constructed.

2.2 Overtly Intrusive Narrators and Authors

Narratorial or authorial intrusions are also quite common in metafictive picturebooks (Hunt 1999: 142). Narrators or authors frequently comment on their own narration or story, for example in the form of disclaimers. On the back cover of Novak's *The Book With No Pictures* (2014), the (adult) reader who presumably reads the book to the kid is warned against its content:

> WARNING! This books looks serious but it is actually COMPLETELY RIDICULOUS! If a kid is trying to make you read this book, the kid is playing a trick on you. You will end up saying SILLY THINGS and making everybody LAUGH AND LAUGH! Don't say I didn't warn you ... (Novak 2014).

This warning on the back of the book subverts the usual back cover text, which gives a hint of the story in an attractive way. This breaking of boundaries helps to distance the reader from the text. Emily Gravett points even more directly to the constructedness of her story, when, on one of the last pages of *Wolves*, she states that the book should not be mistaken for reality:

> The author would like to point out that no rabbits were eaten during the making of this book. It is a work of fiction (Gravett, 2005).

In some metafictive picturebooks, the author even becomes part of the narrative. In *Chloe and the Lion* (Barnett/Rex 2012), the author and the illustrator jointly start off telling Chloe's story, when they suddenly disagree and enter the narrative to discuss how Chloe's story should continue. Rather than being a simple adventure story, this book therefore reflects in a humorous way upon the complex process of creating picturebooks, which requires collaborative efforts of the author and the illustrator.

> Well, look. The fact is I don't really care what **YOU** think. **I'm** the author of this book. You're the illustrator. That means I'm in charge of what happens, and you draw whatever I tell you (Barnett/Rex, 2012).

In other picturebooks, the author or narrator makes the reader part of the story. In *Do Not Open This Book* by Michaela Muntean (2006), the reader is the antagonist who ignores the warning in the title by opening the book. When the reader opens the book, s/he is confronted with a pig who is trying to write a story. With every page turn, however, the reader disturbs the pig which is getting more and more frustrated. The pig enters in a dialogue with the reader:

> Excuse me, but who do you think you are, opening this book when the cover clearly says DO NOT OPEN THIS BOOK!? If a sign on a door reads DO NOT ENTER, do you enter? (Muntean, 2006).

Also in *The Perfectly Messed Up Story* by Patrick McDonnell (2014), the reader is responsible for the mess caused in the story. While reading the perfect story of Louie, the reader seemingly drops jelly and peanut butter on the book, thus messing up the young boy's story. But the reader is also the one who keeps the story going: Because s/he is still present and reading, even though the story is far from being perfect, it can go on and end on a positive note.

By commenting on the content of the story, stepping into or out of stories, or directly addressing the reader, the narrator or author draws attention to the act of narration. This shows the reader that the story is exactly that – a story.

2.3 Characters Transgressing the Narrative Level

In some picturebooks, the characters are aware of the fact that they are part of a book or story. In *This Book Just Ate My Dog* by Richard Byrne (2014), for example, the little girl Bella who »was taking her dog for a stroll across the page« reports that this book just ate her dog. She, therefore, clearly knows that she is in a book.

In many metafictive picturebooks, characters also address the readers and ask for reader agency and involvement. When Bella's dog, the people who come for her help, and finally even Bella herself disappear into the gutter of the book, Bella writes a short letter to the reader to ask her/him for help. The reader has to become active and shake the book to make all the characters finally reappear.

> Dear reader,
> It would be lovely if you could kindly HELP US!
> Please turn this book on its side and SHAKE ...Bella x (Byrne, 2014).

Breaking literary conventions also occurs when characters step out of or into stories. In Gravett's *Wolves* (2005), the reader is confronted with both the primary narrative of Rabbit's world and the secondary narrative of the world of the wolves, outlined in the non-fiction book Rabbit is reading. While Rabbit is reading the book, he gets so immersed in the story that he eventually enters the storyworld of the wolves. Thus, in the course of the picturebook, borders between the two are »breached through metaleptic transgression« (Allan 2012: 81), and both narratives converge. Even the reader is no longer certain what really happened in the story and what was only imagined.

2.4 Paper Engineering

Many picturebooks are constructed in such a way that they are interactive: Readers are required to lift flaps, press somewhere, pull tabs or feel textures. Emily Gravett's *Wolves* (2005), for example, includes the rabbit's library book containing a little library card that can be pulled out. In addition, an envelope with an overdue library notice is stuck into the back of the book which can be opened by the reader. According to Lewis (2001: 98), books which make use of paper engineering are »metafictive to the extent that they tempt readers to withdraw attention from the story [...] in order to look at, play with and admire the paper engineering.«

2.5 Alternative Endings

Some picturebooks offer open or alternative endings. In this way, they resist »traditional forms of narrative closure« (Lewis 2001: 94). Gravett, for example, inserts an ending for »more sensitive readers«, which, however, is slightly unbelievable because it is made of ripped-up pieces of the book.

> Luckily this wolf was a vegetarian, so they shared a jam sandwich, became the best of friends, and lived happily ever after (Gravett, 2005).

Other books such as McDonnell's *A Perfectly Messed-up Story* »loop back to the beginning in a continuous circle« (Lewis 2001: 94). Because of the naughty reader who drops jelly and peanut butter on the pages, four attempts are necessary to tell Louie's story. Every attempt starts with »Once upon a time, little Louie went skipping merrily along.« The last attempt is successful, but it comes to an abrupt end. It is open to the readers' imagination how the story could continue.

2.6 Playful Subversion of Linguistic Conventions

Metafictive picturebooks may also play with language. Thematic wordplay, for example, is quite common. In *Wolves*, rabbit burrows[2] the book from the WEST BUCKS PUBLIC BURROWING LIBRARY, and the book was written by Emily Grrrabbit. Gravett here plays with words of the semantic field 'rabbits' and transfers them into the book/library setting.

In other books, words were subsequently added. The title of »A Perfect Story« was changed with coloured pencils to »A Perfect**ly Messed-up** Story«. Similarly, in *This Book Ate My Dog* the label »This book belongs to _____«, which can be found in many children's books, was altered to »This **naughty** book belongs to_____«. These changes, which were seemingly made by a child, hint at the fact that a story may be modified at any time and thus reflect upon the process of story creation.

A number of metafictive picturebooks also contain nonsense sentences or sound words. This playful subversion of linguistic conventions once again foregrounds the physicality of texts.

---

2   Reference to *burrow*, i.e. a hole in the ground dug by an animal such as a rabbit, especially to live in.

GLUURR-GA-WOCKO ma GRUMPH-a-doo AiiEE! AiiEE! AiiEE!!! BRROO-OOOOGBRROOOOOOGBRROOOOOOG (Novak, 2014).

2.7 Intertextuality and Parody

A number of metafictive picturebooks include intertextual linkages or parodies of specific texts. Such techniques also draw attention to the ways in which fiction is constructed and thereby distance the readers from the text presented. It is usually their aim »to poke fun at the conventions, manners and affectations of a particular genre« (Lewis 2001: 97). Fairy tales are the most frequently parodied texts. In *Chloe and the Lion*, the young girl Chloe, for example, encounters a number of different characters from other works of classic literature such as the woodcutter from *Little Red Riding Hood*.

In Wolves, references to fairy tales can also be found. Wolves are actually the antagonists of many fairy tales (cf. *Little Red Riding Hood, The Three Little Pigs*). Children, therefore, already have some knowledge concerning big bad wolves, which influences their expectations and the interpretation of wolf stories in general. Gravett's *Wolves*, however, plays with this big bad wolf image and presents facts about these animals in a comparatively dry manner (in form of a nonfiction story-within-the-story). In this picturebook, wolves do not eat old ladies or little girls but deer, bison, moose, beavers, voles and rabbits (Gravett 2005).

3 Why Use Metafictive Picturebooks in the EFL Classroom?

A number of studies by Canadian researcher Sylvia Pantaleo (2002, 2004, 2008) have looked into how young readers understand metafictive picturebooks and relate to them. Her findings show that young children are already quite comfortable with metafictive strategies and can use them in their own responses to the texts. Although these studies have been conducted with English native speakers and speakers of English as a second language, metafictive picturebooks can be considered a rich resource for the EFL classroom as well. They can be used with students of different ages and levels of language proficiency, and they playfully invite the readers to participate. Moreover, they help to demonstrate how narratives work by drawing attention to the text as a text, thereby fostering critical reading.

3.1 Motivating for Students of Different Ages and Language Proficiency

Due to their multilayered nature, metafictive picturebooks can be used in different school types and at different levels. Some can already be employed in primary school (e.g. *This Book Just Ate My Dog*, *The Jacket*, *A Perfectly Messed-up Story*). They are particularly suitable for reading aloud and can be reread several times focusing on different levels of the narrative. The verbal text of the books is usually short and therefore does not cause any language overload for the students at lower levels. Some metafictive picturebooks, however, can only fully be appreciated by students in secondary school (e.g. *Wolves*, *Chloe and the Lion*). The complex interaction between images and text as well as the subversion of literary conventions create information gaps which need to be filled by the readers. This requires a certain level of literary and interpretive competence: »Due to their more developed cognitive skills, slightly older L2 students can gain confidence in being perceptive and confident 'gap' readers despite their limited English« (Bland 2013: 130). Thus, many of the metafictive picturebooks can also be used in lower secondary school grades.

3.2 Inspiring Playful Dealing with Language and Literature

Metafictive picturebooks are particularly suitable for the EFL classroom because of their playful character, which contributes to the fun factor in the classroom. They can stimulate a playful way of dealing with literature and language. Linguistic and literary devices such as nonsense sentences, puns and onomatopoeia plus irony and parody add humour to the stories. This can also encourage students to experiment and play with language structures. Due to their participatory character, many metafictive picturebooks actually invite readers to become active themselves and treat the text as a »semiotic playground« (Pantaleo/Sipe 2008: 3). Those texts are therefore great models for creative writing and offer many other possibilities for creativity in the classroom.

3.3 Learning about Literature and Literary Devices

When dealing with literary texts at school, students should develop an understanding of the characteristics of different literary genres and learn about literary and stylistic devices. Metafictive picturebooks are especially helpful to foster students' literary competence.

Before students can understand that certain literary conventions are subverted, they first have to know them and develop a general understanding of how literary texts are constructed – if you want to break the rules, you must first understand them. In some of the metafictive picturebooks, meaning arises from intertextuality or parody and therefore students need to have some knowledge of the original texts in order to understand and appreciate the parody or intertextual reference (Lazar 2015: 99). Thus, it is important to prepare students in the pre-reading phase for the reading experience, to talk about their expectations and to refer back to their prior knowledge concerning literary conventions. As Lewis (2001: 91) notes

> [w]e expect a well-constructed, well-told story to have [...] a beginning, a middle and an end. We expect to find more or less convincing characters interacting in an imaginary world according to the dictates of a plot which the author usually takes the trouble to resolve in some more or less satisfying way.

We realise very quickly when rules are broken and our expectations are unsettled. Thus, by playing with literary conventions and transgressing boundaries, metafictive devices make the conventions and strategies of fiction visible. Metafictive picturebooks make use of a broader range of narrative techniques than the majority of fiction written for children and positions the readers »in a more active interpretive role« (McCallum 2004: 587). McCallum further states that »[b]y involving readers in the production of textual meanings, metafictions can implicitly teach literary and cultural codes and conventions, as well as specific interpretative strategies and hence empower readers to read more competently« (ibid.: 588).

Thus, in metafictive picturebooks students' attention is drawn to how text creation and meaning creation work. In a first step, the students should learn to detect metafictive strategies, and in a second step experiment and try to use some of those strategies in their own writing. Through this engagement with metafiction, students' awareness of the complexities of fiction is sharpened, and they can gain confidence in dealing with any form of text.

3.4 Drawing Attention to the Text as Text

Picturebooks with metafictive devices pose questions about the relationship between fiction and reality. Through the transgression of boundaries and subversion of literary conventions, readers become aware of the fictional nature of the story and understand that fiction does not equal reality.

Emily Gravett's *Wolves* reflects upon the phenomenon of getting lost in a story: Rabbit gets so immersed in the story that he eventually enters the storyworld of the wolves. While he is reading about the bushy tail and the dense fur, he simultaneously walks up the tail and along the back of the wolf until he reaches the nose. Then the text says:

> An adult wolf has 42 teeth. Its jaws are twice as powerful as those of a large dog. Wolves eat mainly meat. They hunt large prey such as deer, bison and moose. They also enjoy smaller mammals, like beavers, voles and ... rabbits (Gravett, 2005).

In the case of this picturebook, Rabbit's complete identification with the story brings the narrative to a tragic conclusion: Rabbit is eaten by the wolves (at least initially, according to its original ending).

Stories as such also reflect upon the »real« world: »Contemporary metafictional writing is both a response and a contribution to an even more thorough-going sense that reality or history are provisional: no longer a world of eternal verities but a series of constructions, artifices, impermanent structures« (Waugh 1987: 7).

3.5 Fostering Critical Reading Skills

Getting immersed in a story and forgetting about everything else is what makes reading such a special experience for many. However, it is also very important to learn to read critically. Metafictive picturebooks invite readers to ask questions, to participate and to think. They contain multiple narrative strands, offer open or alternative endings, and show a high degree of ambiguity and uncertainty. For a real understanding, unreflecting and naïve reading are not effective here; instead the readers have to read between the lines and reflect upon what they are reading. Multiple interpretations by readers are generated.

Another possibility for reflection concerns the power of stories and books: By discussing different metafictive strategies, students can become aware of the ways literary texts manipulate the readers. In our contemporary world, students are constantly exposed to different text types which they have to read and interpret. Therefore, fostering their critical engagement with both written and visual texts should be part of their education. This will have a lasting effect on the students:

> The growing lack of belief or confidence in metanarratives [...] demands a balancing opportunity for empowerment through education, specifically through a literature apprenticeship, to read the world critically, constructively and purposefully, with the pedagogical promise of being able to in-

fluence outcomes at least to some extent and therefore have choices in life
(Bland 2013: 111 f.).

4 Activities with Metafictive Picturebooks

In the following, some pre-/while-/post-reading activities will be suggested
which can be used with metafictive picturebooks in the EFL classroom.

4.1 Pre-Reading Activities

Before the reading process, story conventions and the storytelling process
should be looked into. Students can talk about their prior knowledge concerning
literary rules and discuss their expectations of the text. The following questions
could be raised: »What makes a good story?«, »How does a story work?«, »Can
a story have any ending?« Even primary school pupils can already list some
basic characteristics of stories they are familiar with. Secondary school students
can additionally think of ways in which a story could be changed or retold, and
how it might be played with. They may already be familiar with some stories
which subvert literary conventions, and they can talk about them.

4.2 While-Reading Activities

While reading the story, students are asked to detect metafictive devices. They
can, for example, look for elements which belong to the story-within-the-story
and for those which concern the story itself. In this process, the illustrations
should also be considered. In *Wolves*, for example, Rabbit's world is presented
in cream, whereas the non-fiction elements about wolves are painted in black
and white. When Rabbit becomes more immersed in the story, the cream colour
becomes less, and black and white colouring increases. Analysing the pictures
helps the students to understand how the narrative strands are presented in
the story.

Another aspect of the picturebooks which can be analysed is how language is
used in the text. Students should look for puns and sound words, and they can
also experiment with language themselves.

4.3 Post-Reading Activities

In the post-reading phase, there is considerable scope for creative activities. In primary school, pupils can draw their own illustrations (e.g. of something else which has been eaten by the book in *This Book Just Ate My Dog*), or they can handicraft their own book jacket (*The Jacket*). Secondary school students may express their creativity using words. Possible creative writing activities include finishing a story, rewriting the story from another perspective, writing parallel stories or alternative endings for the stories.

Another post-reading activity for secondary school students could be a classroom discussion on imagination versus reality. A possible starting point is a painting which combines both realistic and imaginary elements[3]. Students could address some of the following questions: »What is imagination?«, »What fires our imagination?«, »Can imagination and reality always be clearly distinguished?« Then they can also look for realistic and imaginary elements in the picturebook(s).

5 Conclusion

Metafictive picturebooks can fulfil multiple purposes in the EFL classroom. Due to their multilayered nature, they can be used with students of different ages and levels of language proficiency. They provide opportunities for playful engagement with language and literary conventions and draw attention to the text as a text. Metafictive picturebooks frequently ask for readers' agency and involvement and thereby foster students' critical reading skills. They provide a welcome change to classroom routine and can increase students' general interest in reading and literature.

Bibliography

Allan, Cherie (2012). Playing with Picturebooks: Postmodernism and the Postmodernesque.Basingstoke: Palgrave Macmillan.

Bland, Janice (2013). Children's Literature and Learner Empowerment: Children and Teenagers in English Language Education. London: Bloomsbury.

Byrne, Richard (2014). This Book Just Ate My Dog! Oxford: Oxford University Press.

Gravett, Emily (2005). Wolves. London: Macmillan Children's Books.

Hall, Kirsten (2014). The Jacket. New York: Enchanted Lion Books.

---

3   For example, one could choose one of Ben Heine's »Pencil vs Camera« artworks, in which the artist mixes photography with drawing.

Hunt, Peter (1999). Understanding Children's Literature: Key Essays from the Second Edition of the International Companion of Children's Literature. London/New York: Routledge.

Lazar, Gillian (2015). Playing with Words and Pictures: Using Post-modernist Picture Books as a Resource with Teenage and Adult Language Learners. In: Teranishi, Masayuki/Saitō, Yoshifumi/Wales, Katie (eds.). Literature and Language Learning in the EFL Classroom. Hampshire/NewYork: Palgrave Macmillan, 94–111.

Lewis, David (2001). Reading Contemporary Picturebooks: Picturing Text. New York: Routledge.

McCallum, Robyn (2004). Metafictions and Experimental Work. In: Hunt, Peter (ed.). International Companion Encyclopedia of Children's Literature. Vol. 1. Oxon/New York: Routledge, 587–598.

McDonnell, Patrick (2014). A Perfectly Messed-Up Story. New York/Boston: Little, Brown and Company.

Muntean, Michaela (2006). Do Not Open This Book! New York: Scholastic Press.

Novak, Benjamin (2014). The Book with No Pictures. New York: Dial Books for Young Readers.

Pantaleo, Sylvia (2002). Grade 1 Students Meet David Wiesner's Three Pigs. Journal of Children's Literature, 28:2, 72–84.

Pantaleo, Sylvia (2004). Young Children Interpret the Metafictive in Anthony Browne's Voices in the Park. Journal of Early Childhood Literacy, 4:2, 211–233.

Pantaleo, Sylvia (2008). Exploring Student Response to Contemporary Picturebooks. Toronto: University of Toronto Press.

Pantaleo, Sylvia/Sipe, Lawrence (2008). Introduction: Postmodernism and Picturebooks. In: Sipe, Lawrence/Pantaleo, Sylvia (eds.). Postmodern Picturebooks. Play, Parody, and Self-Referentiality. New York: Routledge, 1–8.

Waugh, Patricia (1984). Metafiction: The Theory and Practice of Self-Conscious Fiction. London/New York: Methuen.

Katrin Stadlinger-Kessel

Six Words to Fire Your Imagination

Students' imagination can be fired by six words, i.e. the shortest short story on record. In the following, suggestions for a 45-minute lesson on Hemingway's famous short story at an upper-intermediate level are presented.

1 Ideas for a Lesson Plan

The present curriculum for grade 10 at Bavarian 'Gymnasien' expects students to deal with literary, religious, ethical and philosophical questions and to hone their analytical skills when dealing with these kinds of topics. Beyond that, students are to expand their range of English vocabulary and should be encouraged to clearly communicate their ideas orally and in writing.

One of the genres that I consider most suited to this daunting task is the short story: it is a gateway to literature en miniature as well as a playing field for conversation and for classroom activities of all kinds. Besides, it can be dealt with in the framework of a 45-minute lesson or be expanded in various ways. I believe that there is hardly an English teacher in German classrooms who does not have a favourite short story up his or her sleeve to present to students. In any case, one of mine is the shortest short story on record in the English-speaking world: six words attributed to Ernest Hemingway. Allegedly, some of his friends challenged him to write an entire short story under 10 words, and he actually succeeded in winning the bet. This is what he is said to have written:

> For Sale – Baby Shoes – Never Worn

What is most striking here is the contrast between the factual wording of a classified ad and the emotional impact behind it. This is one of the reasons why people find this story so compelling and why it resonates with students, too. For me as a teacher, there is another big advantage of dealing with it in class: no preparation is necessary in terms of photocopied materials, the only things needed are a blackboard and chalk.

2 Phase One: Lead-in and Warm-up

The lesson for today focuses on the topic of SHORT STORIES, and that is what I write on one of the side blackboards, adding to the heading the three different stages that I plan to deal with: **warm-up, basic elements and example**.

Ill. 1: Board sketch

In order to introduce the class to the topic in a rather playful way, I ask one student to recite the alphabet silently, until another student calls 'Stop!'. The letter reached is written on the board and I encourage the class to name five different words starting with this particular letter: I note them all down, too. The 1–2 minute assignment now is to think up a brief story which includes all these words. The suggestions offered are usually nonsense and cause some laughter, but now and again they are really imaginative: starting out with the words *nightmare – nose – November – negotiation – Ninja*, for example, a student of mine once came up with a little literary cameo: »Last November I had a nightmare: a Ninja wanted to take my life. But we negotiated, and in the end he only took my nose.« (*Thank you, Gregory!*)

Ill. 2: Lead-in

3 Phase Two: Basic Elements of a Short Story

As a rule, students have already been introduced to short texts and short stories in grades 8 and 9. What might have been ignored – or forgotten! – are the basic elements that are to be found in a typical short story and which are instrumental in analysing such a text. That is the reason why I draw a mind map on the board, providing the main key terms of analysis step by step and expecting the students to add the corresponding details on their own. This forces them to listen closely, to focus on the most important information provided either by the teacher or their classmates and to note it down. The mind map on the blackboard looks like this:

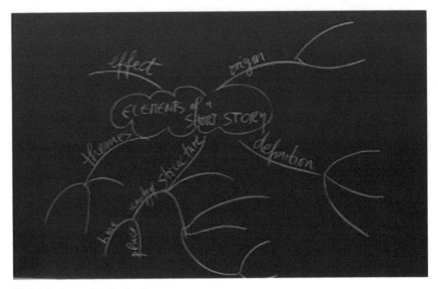

Ill. 3: Mind map (beginning)

At the end of Phase 3, a completed mind map could possibly include all the following details:

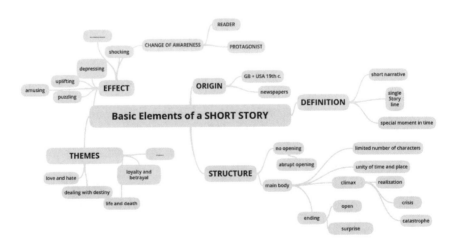

Ill. 4: Mind map (finished)

4 Phase Three: Six Words to Fire your Imagination

Having been provided with the necessary analytical tools, we embark on the most intriguing phase of this lesson: Hemingway's six-word story. I write the six words on the main blackboard ...

> For Sale – Baby Shoes – Never Worn

... and ask the class to reflect on them for a minute, then to turn to their partner and exchange first impressions: *think – pair – share*. A significant number of students actually assume that the baby has died. I ask for suggestions on how that might have happened, and am given answers such as *miscarriage, abortion* or *death at birth*. I draw a small cross on the board and add the ideas we have collected.

As it turns out, the story resonates differently with everyone, and not all the students see the situation as bleak as outlined above. A different explanation for wanting to sell the baby shoes could possibly be a conflict between the mother and the father, or even a separation of the two. Again, I use symbols on the board to keep this idea in mind.

Another, far less dramatic reason for the advertisement could be that one or both parents simply do not want the shoes. A few sketches and words – *wrong size, ugly design, no need* – complement the information collected on the board.

There is a further question I focus on, namely, why a pair of baby shoes is advertised for sale, although their material value is presumably negligible. Could it be that the family lives in dire financial circumstances? Or is it rather a question of an emotional closure for mother and/or father? The shoes could have easily been thrown away, or passed on to a pregnant friend as a gift, but no – they are advertised to be sold. This decision definitely carries more weight and is examined from all sides by the students in my classes.

One last question that can be raised is why Hemingway chose the term 'shoes', and not 'clothes', for example. The association with shoes, of course, is that »they are made for walking«, implying that there is a future to walk towards to – or not. As shown above, new questions lead to a wide range of potential answers, each of which again open up new perspectives.

Saying so much in six words! We can only marvel at Hemingway's masterfully crafted literary jewel, and there is hardly a student in class who is not awed by the number of possibilities for interpretation that it provides. Here we can truly speak of a 'change in awareness', and this term leads us back to the mind map on the board. A brief review of the most essential elements of short stories follows and is referred, point by point, to our short story.

Ill. 5: Story interpretation

5 Phase Four: Creative Activities

Having been offered a variety of interpretations, my students are now encouraged to choose the one they feel most comfortable with and to deal with it in the following ten minutes. I leave it to them to decide whether they prefer to work alone or with a partner, and whether to write down an imaginary dialogue or embark on a role play.

Students have since come up with all sorts of creative responses, ranging from the (melo-)dramatic to the humorous and bizarre, and some have been surprised to experience what unknown resources are tapped and what intuitive ideas surface in their minds.

As for homework, I again give my students a choice: either they deal with the question: *What basic elements of a short story can be found in Hemingway's six words?* and write a brief factual answer. Or I offer them a much more personal approach by encouraging them to write about an incident they experienced as toddlers. As a visual impulse, I hold up the authentic baby shoes that I wore when I first learned to walk. It is the suitable ending to a lesson which has focused on baby shoes and which might just have tugged at your heart strings.

Should you wish to extend the lesson into 90 minutes, a discussion can be initiated on whether the class enjoyed dealing with the short story or not. In preparation, I draw a huge 'smiley' on one half of the black board and a 'frowny' on the other. My students then position themselves accordingly and are asked to justify their views.

Bernard Brown

Short but Sweet!

Motivating Methods of Using Short Texts in the English Lesson

Mr Jones was very happy when the swing that he had ordered for his children finally came in the post. He took the metal parts and nuts and bolts out of the box and his three children looked on excitedly while he tried to put the swing together.

After he had spent a couple of hours reading the assembly instructions and had tried to put the right parts together, poor Mr Jones finally gave up and, in desperation, asked his old neighbour – a talented handyman – to help him.

The neighbor came over, threw away the instructions and assembled the swing in next to no time. Full of admiration, Mr Jones asked him: »How on earth did you manage to put the swing together without even reading the instructions??!«

»To tell you the truth,« the neighbor said, »I can't read and when you can't read, you have to think« (www. jokebuddha.com).

I really feel sorry for that old man: He obviously had the wrong teachers! However I am convinced that no teacher will agree with him: Reading can actually help our thinking skills and vice-versa. The more thinking there is, the more productive and interesting the reading is. In this article I would like to show you a few old and new methods of bringing that certain spark which makes a clear connection between thinking and reading.

One of our goals in the English language lesson should be to give our students the confidence and skills to handle increasingly longer texts. However short texts are often more motivating for our students and allow the teacher to integrate them into a well-rounded lesson and use the texts as a »diving board« for other communicative and interactive activities.

Maze

1. Take an empty maze and with a pencil make a passage through the maze from start to finish. Your path should include all the spaces.
2. Now take a text or excerpt from the text of fifty words and place them in the spaces along the path. If your text contains more than fifty words – as in our example – then you will occasionally need to put two words in some of the spaces.

3. Rub out the pencil marks.
4. Photocopy the maze in the appropriate number.
5. Your students now find their way out of the maze.
6. Now hand out the text or repeat the famous teacher phrase »Turn to page ...«, and the students can see how well they were able to »predict« the text. Our example is based on the leaflet *On Your Bike.*

Such mazes can be easily created in all word processing programmes (tables!). Send me an email (bernard.brown@web.de), and I will send you an empty maze.

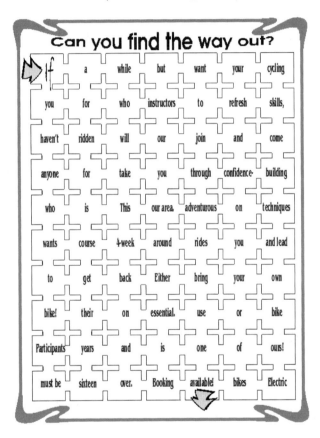

This exercise is a very useful way of teaching students how the parts of a text fit together, i.e. to show them the importance of coherence (how the text makes sense) and cohesion (the way elements of sentences are linked together). (Other examples and empty templates for mazes can be found in Brown 2009, 40–55.) Bernard Brown: *Magic and More: More fun and fascination for the English lesson!* 2009.

Corrupted Texts

This is another motivating method, which gets your students to really burrow into a text like a mole. From one text we make two texts, by adding small mistakes. The correct version of the first sentence is on one of the texts, the incorrect version on the other and so on. It is, of course, important to have an irregular pattern of mistakes e.g. the first mistake in text A, the second mistake in text B, the next two mistakes in text B, etc.

One student gets text A and his partner is given text B. The two students go through the texts together and each time they find two different versions, they decide which version is correct and the student with the incorrect version corrects his sentence accordingly. At the end, both students will have the same text. The teacher hands out the original text and the students check if their corrections were correct.

```
RESTART                                        Text A

Your local Jobcentre is providing special help and advice for people who
                                               is
have been out of work for some time. This was called RESTART.
                                                      been       an
If you have been signing on for six months or more, you may already have invited

your Jobcentre for a RESTART interview. If not you will probably receive an invitation

shortly. Even if you have already had a RESTART interview, you will probably be

invited to call in for further interviews at regular intervals while you are  employed.
```

```
RESTART                                        Text B

Your local Jobcentre is providing special help and advice for people who have been out of work for
         some time
a few days. This is called RESTART.

If you have been signing on for six months or more, you may already have been invited to your
                                                                        shortly
Jobcentre for a RESTART interview. If not you will probably receive an invitation for the weekend. Even if

you have already had a RESTART interview, you will probably be invited to call in for further
                                                         unemployed
interviews at regular intervals while you are employed.
```

RESTART

Text A

Your local Jobcentre is providing special help and advice for people who have been out of work for some time. This was called RESTART.

If you have been signing on for six months or more you may already have invited your Jobcentre for a RESTART interview. If not, you will probably receive an invitation shortly. Even if you have already had a RESTART interview, you will probably be invited to call in for further interviews at regular intervals while you are unemployed.

RESTART gives you the chance to talk with a specialist member of the Jobcentre staff. They can tell you about the jobs, training and other opportunities available in your area. The aim is to give you a job.

Your letter will say where and when you go for your interview. It is important that you go, because that is the only way you can get the help on offer.

If you cannot go at the time given to you, please contact the Jobcentre at once to re-arrange the interview. The address will be on your letter. If you do not go and do not have a good reason, your benefit or credits of National Insurance contributions can be given to you.

If you want to know more about RESTART, or are sure about what to do when your letter arrives, ask the staff at your Benefit Office or Jobcentre. If you haven't been unemployed for six months, but would like advice about ways out of unemployment ask at your Unemployment Benefit Office about the CLAIMANT ADVISER SERVICE.

RESTART

Text B

Your local Jobcentre is providing special help and advice for people who have been out of work for a few days. This is called RESTART.

If you have been signing on for six months or more you may already have been invited to your Jobcentre for a RESTART interview. If not, you will probably receive an invitation for the weekend. Even if you have already had a RESTART interview, you will probably be invited to call in for further interviews at regular intervals while you are employed.

RESTART gives you the chance to talk with a specialist friend of the Jobcentre staff. They can tell you about the jobs, training and other opportunities available in Europe. The aim is to help you towards a job.

Your letter will say how and why you go for your interview. It is not important that you go, because that is not the only way you can get the help on offer.

If you can go at the time given to you, please contact the Jobcentre at once to re-arrange the interview. The telephone number will be on your letter. If you do not go and do not have a good reason, your benefit or credits of National Insurance contributions can be stopped.

If you want to know more about RESTART, or are unsure about what to do when your letter arrives, ask the staff at your Benefit Office or Jobcentre. If you haven't been unemployed for six months, but would like advice about ways to work at a Jobcentre ask at your Unemployment Benefit Office about the CLAIMANT ADVISER SERVICE.

Just one Word!

Take your text and add a word to each sentence. Ask the students to go through the text and cross out the words which are obviously not part of the original text. Then hand out the original text and the students can check if their choices were right or wrong.

There is one word too many in each sentence. Cross out the extra words.

Useful help and advice

Your local Jobcentre is providing special help and advice for old people who have been out of work for some time. This is often called RESTART. If you have been signing on for six months or more you may not have been invited to your Jobcentre for a RESTART interview. If not, you will probably receive an unusual invitation shortly. Even if you have already had a RESTART interview, maybe you will probably be invited to call in for further interviews at regular intervals. While you are unemployed. RESTART gives you the chance to talk quickly with a specialist member of the Jobcentre staff. They can tell you about the jobs, training, restaurants and other opportunities available in your area. The aim is to help you towards a boring job. The letter will not say where and when to go for your interview. It is important that you go, because that is the only interesting way you can get the help on offer. If you cannot go at the time given to you, please contact the Jobcentre at once to re-arrange an interview, sorry. The telephone number will perhaps be on your letter. If you do not go and do not have a good reason, your fantastic benefits or credits of National Insurance contributions can be stopped. If you don't want to know more about RESTART, or are unsure about what to do when your letter arrives, ask the staff at your Benefit Office or Jobcentre. If you haven't been unemployed for six months, but would like advice about ways out of unemployment ask at your Men's Unemployment Benefit Office about the CLAIMANT ADVISER SERVICE.

Removing Punctuation and Capital Letters

where do the punctuation marks and capital letters come in a passage this is a question which the student can only answer if he has understood the text don't you think it is a nice exercise i hope you will try it out dialogues especially can be dealt with in this way.

A more difficult but fun exercise is to not only remove all punctuation marks but also the spaces between the letters. Here is an example of such an exercise.

doyouwanttogetbackonyourbikebutfeelanxiouswouldyouliketorideontheroadbutlackconfidenceifyouhaventriddenforawhilebutwanttorefreshyourcyclingskillscomeandjoinourinstructorswhowilltakeyouthroughconfidencebuildingtechniquesandleadyouonadventurousridesaroundourareathisfourweekcourseisforanyonewhowantstogetontheirbikeparticipantsmustbe16yearsandoverbookingisessential

Three-in-One

This is another example of »doctoring« a text which also encourages the student to read the chosen text very closely. For parts of the text, choose two alternatives. The student chooses the solution which best fits the text:

Choose the most suitable words and expressions in this text:

Useful help and advice

Your local Jobcentre is providing special help and advice for people who have been out of work

a) *for a few days.*　　　a) *can help you and your parents.*
b) *for some time.* 　This b) *is called RESTART.*　　　If you have been signing on
c) *and don't like work*　c) *is a nice place to meet people.*

a) *been invited to*
for six months or more you may have b) *invited*　　　your Jobcentre for a RESTART interview.
c) *read about*

a) *for the weekend.*
If not, you will probably receive an invitation b) *next year.*　　Even if you have already had a
c) *shortly.*

a) *tea and a piece of cake*
RESTART interview, you will probably be invited to call in for b) *more fun*
d) *further interviews at regular intervals*

a) *specialist*
while you are unemployed. RESTART gives you the chance to talk with a b) *talented*　　member of
c) *nice*

the Jobcentre staff. They can tell you about the jobs, training and other opportunities available

a) *Europe.*　　　　　a) *give you a very well-paid job.*
in b) *London.*　The aim is to help you b) *towards a job.*
c) *your area*　　　　c) *show you newspaper ads for a job.*

a) *where and how*
Your letter will say b) *why and where*　to go for your interview. It is important that you go, because
c) *where and when*

a) *from our secretary.*　　a) *would like*
that is the only way you can get the help b) *we need*　　　If you b) *cannot*　　go at the time given
c) *on offer.*　　　　　c) *didn't*

to you, please contact the Jobcentre at once to re-arrange an interview. The telephone number will be

a) *on your letter.*
b) *in the telephone directory.*　If you do not go and do not have a good reason, your benefits or credits of
c) *in most newspapers.*

a) *continued*
National Insurance contributions can be b) *stopped.*
c) *given to you.*

a) *very happy*
If you want to know more about RESTART, or are b) *sure.*　　about what to do when your letter arrives,
c) *unsure.*

ask the staff at your Benefit Office or Jobcentre.

Matching and Sequencing

Matching and sequencing are, of course, classic exercises in foreign language teaching but they still appeal to students and teachers and are an excellent way of testing text comprehension. To master it, the students (in pairs or small groups) have to be able to recognize devices indicating cohesion and/or coherence. The text is photocopied onto coloured paper or (preferably) carton and the parts of the sentences are cut out and put into envelopes. Each pair receives one envelope with the instruction to form seven correct sentences.

A Traineeship is an opportunity for you to get a work placement whilst gaining qualifications	are in for classes.
	when on work placement.
The Traineeship lasts for 12 weeks during which you will attend 2-3 days in an established company	you will have the opportunity to progress onto a paid apprenticeship.
Your travel and lunch will be paid for	to build up your current skills and increase the content on your CV.
The programme will be starting shortly	at the end of your Traineeship!
Once the traineeship is completed	So contact us without delay to reserve your place.
Breakfast provided on the days you	and 2-3 days attending workshops to increase your work skills
Guaranteed interview	

Student Created Gapped Texts

The gap test is another old favourite in language teaching (at least with many teachers!). In the classic cloze test, every seventh word or so is deleted and the student has to find words which fit. An interesting variation is to have the pupils in small groups make their own gapped tests for separate texts or excerpts from texts and have other students find the solutions.

Make a test for other students! Remove ten words in the text with Tip Ex!
Are you –23?
Do you want the right help to get your ...... in the
door and into the .... you want?
Have you .... of doing a Traineeship?
What ..... a traineeship?
A Traineeship is an opportunity for you to get a .... placement whilst gaining ......, to build up your current skills and increase the content on your CV. The Traineeship .... for 12 weeks during which you will attend 2-3 days in an established .... and 2-3 days attending workshops to increase your work.
Now give your text to another group and see if they can guess the words that you have removed. Can you guess the words they have crossed out in their part of the text?

Using the Text as a »Diving Board«

Up to now we have been discussing a few motivating methods of helping students to understand texts. It is a shame that in many EFL lessons the handling of texts is restricted to ascertaining the contents and maybe a few vocabulary exercises based on the text. We really bring the spark into the lesson, however, when the students are asked to go beyond the text – when we use it as a »diving board« for encouraging further thought and other communicative activities. Here are just a few suggestions relating to the texts discussed so far.

Restart: After reading the text, the students are divided into groups. One half of the groups decide what questions they, as members of the staff of Jobcentre, would ask interviewees in a RESTART interview who have been unemployed for some time and write the questions down. (What training have you had? What sort of jobs are you interested in? Do you mind travelling for half-an-hour to your job? What was your last job? etc.) The other groups write down questions interviewees might like to ask the interviewer(s) from Jobcentre. (Where can I train to be a plumber? What jobs can I train for? What are 'credits of National Insurance contributions? etc.) The teacher collects the lists of questions. Each group now gets a list of questions written by a different group and has to decide what answers they would recommend (and would not recommend!). After the results have been discussed in the whole class, some students can be chosen to make a role play of such an interview.

Traineeships: In partner work, the students read the pamphlet Traineeships (see above) and indicate how important they consider each item mentioned: 1 = extremely important (guaranteed interview at end of traineeship? Opportunity to progress onto paid apprenticeship?); 2 = quite important (Your travel and lunch will be paid for when on work placement?); 3 = not so important (Amazon vouchers to spend as you please?). The students discuss their ranking with another pair, giving the reasons for their choices. The group then comes to a group consensus which, at the end of the lesson, it can defend in front of the class.

On your bike: In small groups the students use a given text as a model for a new text that they write. Using the principle of »creative plagiarism«, they can use whole chunks of the original text or only individual words. The text ON YOUR BIKE (see above) can, with a number of modifications, be used to write a text for advertising swimming courses, skate-boarding, table tennis training, etc. Extra details (contact, place, etc.) can also be added. As many of our students are very computer literate, they may enjoy making the leaflets with the help of clip arts and a graphics programme. The finished products can be hung up on the walls and your students can decide which of the activities on offer they would prefer.

C. Lessons

Proverbs & Perverbs

1 Genre

At an average length of seven words (Thaler 2008: 84), proverbs are »short, generally known sentence[s] of the folk which contain [...] wisdom, truth, morals, and traditional views in metaphorical, fixed and memorisable form and which [are] handed down from generation to generation« (Mieder 1989: 119).

Sabban (1991: 83) distinguishes two types of proverb variation: expression variants ('Ausdrucksvarianten') and new creations ('Neuschöpfungen'). Expression variants are proverbs which differ in one or more expressions but keep the same meaning due to the synonymic nature of the varying words. It follows that *anti-proverbs,* or *perverbs,* have to belong to the category of new creations, since they are »the results of deliberate proverb innovations that may or may not negate the truth of the original piece« (Litovkina/Mieder 2006: 58i). These innovations can be substitutions of essential parts of an existing proverb or reversions of its original meaning. In most cases, the original structure remains the same, since aspects like »alliteration, rhyme, paronomasia, metaphor and many others [...] are very effective for carrying different ideas to the society in a very compact form [and thus] provide the possibility of making changes in traditional English proverbs« (Valdeva 2003: 379). Simply put, *anti-proverbs* are proverbs commonly used or created to humorous purposes, dealing with modern-day topics like religion, feminism, politics, inter-sex relations and others (Valdeva 2003). Among the various phonetic, syntactic, and lexical stylistic devices for creating *anti-proverbs*, Thaler (2008: 84) states reduction, supplementation, substitution, contrast and synthesis as the most prominent ones.

Gözpinar (2014: 612) follows Mieder's argumentation that the importance of proverbs lies in their belonging to the »common knowledge of basically all native speakers«, used to communicate about wisdom, human nature and the entire world. The majority of teachers who participated in her study confirmed the suitability of proverbs for learning a new language: they facilitate effective communication and the understanding of humor, help with language education in general and result in »improved oral presentation effectiveness, improved reading skills, improved written communication skills, [and] improved listening and comprehension« (Gözpinar 2014: 616). Since anti-proverbs are basically more modern, humorous forms of traditional proverbs, they should be taught along with them.

2 Procedure

Text	Collection of proverbs from different fields of life
Competences	Reading, speaking, creative writing, language awareness
Topics	Miscellaneous on life, folk wisdom, proverbs and perverbs, rhetorical devices
Level	Intermediate
Time	90 minutes (or shorter: each of the tasks can be integrated in a different lesson)

Steps

A. Lead-in
1. Teacher (T) presents the proverb »the pen is mightier than the sword« with the help of a picture (cf. Materials 1).
2. Discussion: What does it mean? Is there a German (French, Italian ...) equivalent? What is this type of saying called?

B. Theory (proverb basics)
1. T provides the definition of proverbs (also mentions anti-proverbs).
2. T gives examples that highlight the importance of proverbs.

C. Practical part I
1. Matching exercise: Students (S) do Worksheet (cf. M 2: Matching Proverbs with their Meaning).
2. T collects answers from students and corrects them if necessary.

D. Theory (rhetorical devices)
1. T hands out Worksheet (cf. M 3: Rhetorical Devices) and collects the key answers with the class.
2. T explains the importance of rhetorical devices and their functions.
3. T hands out Worksheet (cf. M 4: Spot the Rhetorical Devices).

E. Practical part II
1. S get together with their neighbours and do Worksheet.
2. S pairs share and compare their results with the pair next to them.
3. The whole class collects answers with corrections made by the T.

F. Fillers
1. *Visual proverbs*
S are shown pictures which visualise proverbs (M 5). They have to guess which proverb is depicted. (Alternative: T divides the class into groups and turns the guessing into a game.) If no one knows the answer, language support can be given (4 answers each).
2. *Anti-proverbs*
First S are instructed on the theory of anti-proverbs (M 6, upper part). Then, in pairs, they try to invent an anti-proverb.
3. *Collection*
T hands out a sheet with a collection of proverbs for further use: Worksheet (M 7, possibly: test in the following lesson).

G. Homework
Option 1: S are asked to write a short story that has a proverb/anti-proverb as its moral.
Option 2: S write a story or poem in which they include as many rhetorical devices as possible.

Follow-up Lesson
At the beginning of the following lesson, stories and poems are read out, with the other S guessing the correct proverbs or rhetorical devices.

3 Materials

M 1: The pen is mightier than the sword

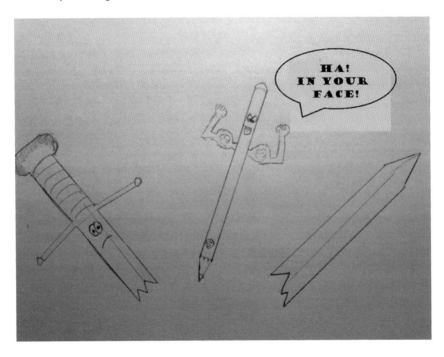

M 2: Matching proverbs with their meaning

	Proverb		Meaning
1	A flower blooms more than once.	A	One should learn from one's mistakes.
2	The best advice is found on the pillow.	B	When two people do s.th. together, one will be the leader.
3	Every cloud has a silver lining.	C	A bad parent does not raise good children.
4	Fool me once, shame on you; fool me twice, shame on me.	D	It is wrong to harm s.o. because they harmed you.

5	You can lead a horse to water, but you can't make it drink.	E	If you miss an occasion, you can avail yourself of it another time.
6	Two wrongs don't make a right.	F	If you don't work, you won't have anything when you're old.
7	A bad tree does not yield good apples.	G	Every good thing has an unpleasant side.
8	If two ride a horse, one must ride behind.	H	There is a positive or hopeful side to every situation.
9	Better lose the saddle than the horse.	I	A good night's sleep helps us find an answer to our problem.
10	A young idler, an old beggar.	J	You can offer s. o. an opportunity to do s. th. but you can't force them to actually do it.
11	Every rose has its thorn.	K	It's better to accept a small loss than risk losing everything.

M 3: Rhetorical devices

Device	Explanation	Examples
1. Alliteration	Repetition of initial vowel or consonant sound	
2. Anaphora	Successive phrases/clauses starting with the same word	
3. Antithesis	Contrast within parallel phrases	
4. Assonance	Repetition of vowel sounds	
5. Ellipsis	Omission of a word/short phrase	
6. Metaphor	Identifying s.th. as being the same as some unrelated thing	
7. Metonymy	A thing is called not by its own name but by the name of s.th. associated in meaning with it	
8. Parallelism	Similar construction in phrases or sentences	
9. Personification	Presenting ideas, objects, animals as persons	

| 10. Simile | Comparison of two different things using *like* or *as* | |

Examples

a. The orders came from the White House.
b. The rain in Spain stays mainly on the plain.
c. We shall not flag or fail. We shall go on to the end. We shall fight in France; we shall fight on the seas.
d. The wind softly kissed my cheek.
e. What you see is what you get.
f. You're as cold as ice.
g. John forgives Mary and Mary, John.
h. Man proposes, God disposes.
i. All the world's a stage.
j. Safe and sound.

M 4: Spot the rhetorical devices

Task

Take a look at the proverbs below. Each of them contains at least one rhetorical device. Find it and write it in the right column of the table.

Rhetorical Devices

alliteration, anaphora, antithesis, assonance, ellipsis, metaphor, metonymy, parallelism, personification, simile

Proverbs	Rhetorical Device
1. A penny saved is a penny earned.	
2. All roads lead to Rome.	
3. All that glitters is not gold.	
4. Practice makes perfect.	
5. Deeds, not words.	
6. Easy come, easy go.	
7. Failure is the mother of success.	
8. Faults are thick where love is thin.	
9. The pen is mightier than the sword.	
10. Spend money like water.	

M 5: Visual proverbs

(a) »A bird in the hand will fly to a bush«
(b) »A bird in the hand will never be as happy as birds in the bush«
(c) »A bird in the hand is worth two in the bush«
(d) »A bird in the hand should be put in a bush«

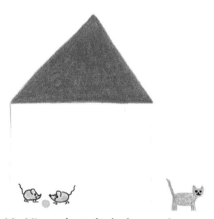

(a) »Mice and cats don't play together«
(b) »When the cat's away, the mice will play«
(c) »Two mice are mightier than a cat«
(d) »When the cat is outside the mice will go wild«

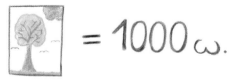

(a) »A picture is worth a thousand words«
(b) »A picture can be described with a thousand words«
(c) »A picture is better than a thousand words«
(d) »A picture is worse than a thousand words«

(a) »Two wrong people will never get anything right«
(b) »Math doesn't make any sense«
(c) »Two wrongs don't make a right«
(d) »Two no's will never equal a yes«

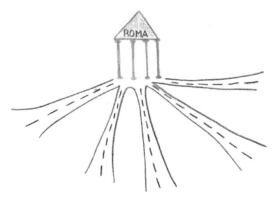

(a) »All roads lead away from Rome«
(b) »All roads lead to Rome«
(c) »All roads end in Rome«
(d) »All roads are in Rome«

(a) »Too many cooks spoil the broth«
(b) »The more cooks the better the broth«
(c) »Cooking in a group will spoil the food«
(d) »Too many cooks means too much salt in the soup«

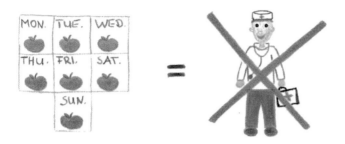

(a) »An apple a day can't keep the doctor away«
(b) »An apple a day means the doctor will stay«
(c) »An apple a day scares doctors away«
(d) »An apple a day keeps the doctor away«

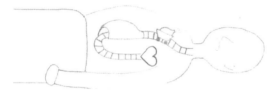

(a) »The way to a man's heart is through his stomach«
(b) »The only thing a man truly loves is food«
(c) »You can't trust a man who doesn't like chicken«
(d) »Women who let you sleep to digest are the best«

(a) »Not every egg gets you a chicken«
(b) »An egg not eaten is a wasted egg«
(c) »Don't count your chickens before they're hatched«
(d) »Some chickens hatch faster than others«

(a) »Brain always triumphs over strength«
(b) »If you can handle a pen you'll never need a sword«
(c) »The pen is smarter than the sword«
(d) »The pen is mightier than the sword«

(a) »Everyone starts small«
(b) »Great oaks from little acorns grow«
(c) »The bigger the tree the smaller the fruit it yields«
(d) »The more time you spend growing, the mightier you'll be«

(a) »The early bird catches the worm«
(b) »Being late only holds disadvantages«
(c) »The early bird is successful«
(d) »He who rises early will be rewarded«

(a) »Love is nothing you see, it's something you feel«
(b) »Love sees with the heart«
(c) »Seeing with your heart is purer than seeing with your eyes«
(d) »Love is blind«

(a) »The richer you are the more lonesome you feel«
(b) »Money isn't everything«
(c) »You can buy your way off of any island«
(d) »Money on an island is as useful as a match in a fire«

M 6: Anti-proverbs

Perverbs	
An *anti-proverb* / *perverb* is the transformation of a standard proverb for humorous effect. Transformation may appear in various patterns:	
1. Reduction	All's well that ends.
2. Supplementation	A barking dog never bites, but a lot of dogs don't know this proverb.
3. Substitution	The best things in life are for a fee.
4. Contrast	All we need is love – all we get is homework.
5. Break of metaphor	Duty is calling? We call back.
6. Synthesis	Marriages are made in heaven knows what state of mind.
Now, in pairs, try to create your own anti-proverb. You may take any proverb you like as a starting point, and any of the six structural patterns mentioned above.	

M 7: Collection of proverbs

Proverb	Meaning
A bird in the hand is worth two in the bush.	It is better to keep what you have rather than to risk losing it by searching for something better.
A flower blooms more than once.	If you miss an occasion, you can avail yourself of it another time.
A penny saved is a penny earned.	It is as useful to save money that you already have as it is to earn more.
All that glitters is not gold.	Superficial attractiveness may not denote great value.
Better lose the saddle than the horse.	It's better to stop and accept a small loss than continue and risk losing everything.
Deeds, not words.	A person is judged more by his actions than by what he says.
Easy come, easy go.	Things easily acquired may be lost just as easily.

Every cloud has a silver lining.	Every misfortune has its bright side.
Every rose has its thorn.	Every good thing has an unpleasant side.
Failure is the mother of success.	Failing is often a stepping stone towards being successful.
Faults are thick where love is thin.	Mistakes made by people you don't truly like are unlikely to be forgiven.
Fool me once, shame on you; fool me twice, shame on me.	One should learn from one's mistakes.
Practice makes perfect.	Doing something repeatedly is the only way to become good at it.
Spend money like water	To spend too much money in a careless way

4 Solutions

A.2.
»The pen is mightier than the sword«: trying to convince people with ideas and words is better than trying to force people to do what you want, German equivalent: »Die Feder ist mächtiger als das Schwert«, type of saying: proverb

B.1.
- A proverb is a short, generally known sentence of the folk. It contains wisdom, truth and morals. It is easily memorable and is passed on from generation to generation.
- Anti-Proverbs are transformations of existing proverbs (alterations, parodies, etc.), usually having a humorous effect.

B.2.
Importance:
- Proverbs reveal something about the respective culture, form an important part of everyday conversation, play a role in raising children
- Proverbs are omnipresent:
    - Eminem song: »Ha! I got some skeletons in my closet«
    - Harry Potter books/movies (anti-proverbs): Dumbledore: »It's no good crying over spilt potion«, »Don't count your owls before they are delivered«
    - Advertisements: »Not only absence makes the heart grow fonder« (Godiva Chocolatier)

M 2:
1–E, 2–I, 3–H, 4–A, 5–J, 6–D, 7–C, 8–B, 9–K, 10–F, 11–G

M 3:
1j, 2c, 3h, 4b, 5g, 6i, 7a, 8e, 9d, 10f

D.2.
Functions of rhetorical devices: play a crucial role in almost any piece of literature, serve to emphasize a certain aspect, arouse reader's attention, criticise a
person/situation/idea, produce rhythm, create humour, trigger mental images,
make passages vivid, surprise the reader

M 4:
1. Parallelism
2. Assonance
3. Metaphor
4. Alliteration
5. Ellipsis
6. Anaphora, parallelism
7. Personification
8. Antithesis
9. Metonymy
10. Simile

G. Homework

1. Short Stories
Once, Jesus had the plan to serve the poor people begging at the temple a de-
licious soup. He and his friends spent the whole afternoon preparing it. When
they were done, they brought the pot to the temple only to find that they had
forgotten the spoons to eat the soup with. They were about to panic when one
of the beggars told them that they might just as well drink the broth straight
from their bowls. »You're right!« Jesus said happily. »After all, it's better to lose
the ladle than the broth.«
(Anti-Proverb: *It's better to lose the ladle than the broth*;
Original Proverb: *It's better to lose the saddle than the horse*)

2. Poems

Homework is stupid, homework is bad	anaphora, parallelism, personification
Homework I hate you, you make me so mad	personification
You are like a monster that haunts me all day	simile
I wish you'd just leave me and stay away	personification

Bibliography

Brainlesstales. http://www.brainlesstales.com/2012-01-03/the-mighty-pen. (28/08/2015)

Englische Grammatik Online. https://www.ego4u.de/de/cram-up/writing/style. (28/08/2015)

Gözpinar, Halis (2014). English Teacher's Interest in Proverbs in Language Teaching. The Journal of International Social Research 7:31. 611–617.

Harris, Robert (2013). A Handbook of Rhetorical Devices. http://www.virtual-salt.com/rhetoric.htm. (28/08/2015)

Learn English Today. http://www.learn-english-today.com/proverbs/proverbs. html. (28/08/2015)

Literary Devices. http://literarydevices.net. (28/08/2015)

Litovkina, Anna/Mieder, Wolfgang (2006). Old Proverbs Never Die, They just Diversify. Burlington/Veszprem: University of Vermont & University of Veszprem.

Mieder, Wolfgang (1989). American Proverbs: A Study of Texts and Contexts. New York: Lang.

Mieder, Wolfgang (1993). Proverbs are Never out of Season. Popular Wisdom in the Modern Age. Oxford: Oxford University Press.

PhraseMix. http://www.phrasemix.com/collections/the-50-most-important-english-proverbs. (28/08/2015)

Sabban, Annette (1991). 'Die dümmsten Bauern haben nicht mehr die dicksten Kartoffeln' – Variationen von Sprichwörtern im und als Text. In: Sabban, Annette/Wirrer, Jan (eds.) Sprichwörter und Redensarten im interkulturellen Vergleich. Opladen: Westdt. Verlag, 83–108.

SoftSchools. http://www.softschools.com/examples/grammar. (28/08/2015)

Thaler, Engelbert (2008). Teaching English Literature. Paderborn: Schöningh.

Thaler, Engelbert (2012). Englisch unterrichten. Grundlagen – Kompetenzen – Methoden. Berlin: Cornelsen.

The Phrase Finder. http://www.phrases.org.uk/meanings/proverbs.html.
   (28/08/2015)
Valdeva, Tatiana (2003). Anti-Proverbs or New Proverbs: The use of English
   Anti-Proverbs and their Stylistic Analysis. Proverbium 20, 379–390.
Your Dictionary. http://examples.yourdictionary.com/examples-of-rhetorical-
   devices.html. (28/08/2015)

Anecdotes

1 Genre

An anecdote is a brief tale narrating an interesting or amusing biographical incident (Cuddon 1992: 42; Thaler 2008). It is based on real life and involves real people, in real places, but due to retelling often becomes a fictional piece, which looks »too good to be true«.

Although mostly humorous, the intention of an anecdote is not only to arouse laughter, as is the case with jokes. Anecdotes, in addition, often reveal some general truth, unveil the workings of an institution, or delineate a character trait.

According to a famous quote by Novalis, an anecdote »is a historical element«. A brief monologue beginning »People are often bored by the tedious small talk ...« will be a joke. A brief monologue beginning »Roosevelt was often bored by the tedious small talk ...« will be an anecdote. Thus an anecdote is close to a parable, but is also distinct from it in the historical specificity it claims.

The word *anecdote* derives from Greek 'anekdota', meaning »things unpublished« (www.etymonline.com). Procopius of Caesarea, the biographer of Justinian I, produced a work entitled Ἀνέκδοτα (Anekdota, translated as »Unpublished Memoirs or Secret History«), which is a collection of short incidents from the private life of the Byzantine court. Gradually, the term *anecdote* came to be applied to any short tale used to illustrate whatever point the author intended to make.

2 Procedure

Text	Anecdote about F. D. Roosevelt (author unknown): »I murdered my grandmother« (www.history.inrebus.com)
Synopsis	Franklin D. Roosevelt indulges in inappropriate small talk with guests at a social function and receives a witty answer from one of his guests.
Competences	Reading, speaking, intercultural communicative competence, text competence, lexical competence

Topics	Small talk, American President, US politics, humour, quick-witted-ness
Level	Intermediate
Time	45 minutes (or 90': with »quick at repartee«)

Steps (global-to-detail approach):

1. Lead-in
a) T shows a picture of Roosevelt (Material 1), has S describe it, explains unknown vocabulary (e.g. *polio, President, wheelchair, Oval Office*).
b) T gives background information on FDR (President of the United States, first President to serve more than two terms, sickness / polio, wheelchair ...)

2. First reading
T reads out the anecdote (M 2: transparency).

3. Global comprehension
T asks about the punch-line. The phrase »she had it coming to her« will have to be explained. S may ask about other unknown words (*tedious, social function* ...).

4. Second reading
3 S read out the anecdote (one narrator, Roosevelt, guest).

5. Detailed comprehension
T and S discuss what is weird about the conversation.

6. Follow-up
a) The topic of *small talk* is elaborated on. A mind map on the characteristics of small talk is developed.
b) The results of the mind map are compared to the contents of the anecdote.

Homework
Choose one of the following tasks:
- Write a formal small talk between Roosevelt and one of his guests.
- Write an informal small talk between you and one of your party guests.
The worksheet with useful phrases (M 3) will help you.

Idea for follow-up lesson:
Quick at repartee (M 4)

3 Materials

M 1:
- One or two photos of Roosevelt (e.g. FDR in his Oval Office, FDR in a wheelchair with child ▸ Google picture search »Roosevelt«) OR
- photo & quote: *Speak soflty and carry a BIG STICK* (www.notable-quotes.com/r/theodore_roosevelt_quote_2.jpg)

M 2: Anecdote
Roosevelt was often bored by the tedious small talk that was required of him at social functions. He often felt as if those with whom he conversed were seldom paying attention to what was said. To prove his point, sometimes Roosevelt would begin a conversation by saying, »I murdered my grandmother this morning.« Often these words were met with polite approval. On one occasion, however, an attentive listener gave the witty reply, »I'm sure she had it coming to her.«
(http://history.inrebus.com/index.php?category=7)

M 3: Language support for small talk

Small Talk: Useful Phrases	
Beginning small talk: Hello, my name is … It's a pleasure to meet you. Hello, how are you? I'd like to indtroduce you to … Pretty nice place, isn't it?	
Continuing small talk:	
Talking about the weather	Beautiful day, isn't it? Can you believe all of this rain we've been having? It looks like it's going to snow. Did you order this sunshine?
Talking about current events	Did you catch the news today? Did you hear about that fire on Fourth St? I read in the paper today that … is closing. How about FC Augsburg? Do you think they're going to win tonight?

At the office	Looking forward to the weekend? Has it been a long week? You look like you could use a cup of coffee.
At a social event	So, how do you know Mary? Have you tried the mince pies? Are you enjoying yourself? It looks like you could use another drink. Your skirt is beautiful. May I ask where you bought it?
Waiting somewhere	I didn't think it would be so busy today. The bus must be running late today. How long have you been waiting?

Ending small talk:
It was nice meeting you.
I have to leave now, but it'd be nice to see you again.
See you later.
Bye, have a good night.

M 4: Repartee

Quick at repartee

1. Example
A beautiful but rather simple-minded woman once asked the famous play-
wright George Bernard Shaw how he would feel about him fathering her child:
»Just imagine a child with your intelligence and my beauty,« she said.
Shaw quickly replied: »Yes, but imagine if it were the other way round!«

2. Definition
Repartee is a quick and witty reply, or an interchange of clever retorts. It
comes from the French fencing word 'repartire', i.e. an answering thrust
with a sword. When you engage in repartee, you do not literally stab someone, but you come back with a quick sharp blow.

3. Relevance
Such a light sparring with words can be very amusing. It is not only in
Britain that a person who is quick at repartee holds high prestige. Having
the right response at the right moment helps you to overcome critical situations, counterattack unfair attacks, and increase the enjoyment of the
conversation.
Becoming witty with words is anything but easy, as Mark Twain realized in
his definition of repartee: »something we think of 24 hours too late.« But
one can work on it.

4. Tasks
a) Monty Python's Oscar Wilde sketch is shown and discussed.
b) A few sample dialogues are presented, and S have to discover parallels.
c) Alternatives to a witty punchline are sought.
d) The last line is left out, and S have to invent their own witty punchline.
e) S only get the punchline, and have to add a suitable first part.
f) In pairs, S try to write another dialogue with a witty end.

5. Example
Constantly swarmed by press and photographers, Gandhi was peppered with
questions wherever he went. One day a reporter yelled out.
»What do you think of Western civilization?«
Gandhi's reply instantly transformed him from an object of curiosity into a
celebrity. In his heavy Indian accent, he answered:
»I think it would be a good idea.«

4 Solutions

Step 5: Detailed comprehension
Roosevelt says he murdered his grandmother – weird remark is answered with
polite approval – witty answer by the guest.

Step 6:
a) Mind map
4 clouds:
- What?
Social conversation/polite/unimportant content
- How?
Three phases (beginning, continuing, ending small talk), avoiding taboo topics
(politics, money, religion), formal and informal, small talk phrases
- Why?
Phatic communication (establishing or keeping up contact), politeness, part of
Anglo-American culture, breaking the ice
- Where?
Parties/when meeting someone/bus stop

b)
- Roosevelt saying he murdered his grandmother ▸ having got tired of small talk,
he wanted to try out s.th different, or he thought people did not listen anyway.
- Weird remark is answered with polite approval ▸ content is not so important
in small talk, or guests are too polite to react in a shocked (amused) manner.
- Funny answer by the guest ▸ punch-line: one guest seriously responded to
what Roosevelt said, or he was trying to be funny.

Bibliography
Cuddon, John (1992). Penguin Dictionary of Literary Terms and Literary The-
    ory. London: Penguin Books.
Thaler, Engelbert (2012). Quick at repartee – Amüsant-kluges Fechten mit Ge-
    danken. PRAXIS Fremdsprachenunterricht 3/12, 18.
Thaler, Engelbert (2008). Teaching English Literature. Paderborn: Schöningh.
www.etymonline.com (30/12/2015)

Urban Myths

1 Genre

»A friend of mine told me …« – that is how urban legends usually begin. These modern folk tales narrate stories which are presumably real, but odd, and supposedly happened to a friend of a friend (Brunvand 1999: 19).

Everyone encounters urban legends in their everyday life. They are told by campfires at summer camp, at the schoolyard, and later at the workplace. One may argue that in the era of Internet & Facebook, urban legends are more widespread than ever before. Whereas traditional folk tales used to be part of regional culture, urban legends can now become global phenomena. They also influence other media, such as commercials, movies and even children's books (Jüngst 1999: 7f.).

Urban legends are considered folklore, and as such their main feature is their circulation in the general population (Brunvand 1988; Brunvand 1999). Further characteristics are the following:

- They sound probable. This feature allows for urban legends to spread. If nobody believed them, they would not be retold and become popular.
- They do not necessarily need to be false. In fact there are a number of urban legends that are true, or a least have a true core, for example the story of the criminals who called the police themselves (www.snopes. com). Stories like that sound probable, but also odd – or as Brunvand (1999) titles his book: *Too Good to Be True.*
- As urban legends are passed on they are continuously revised and altered. Children usually learn about this effect at a very young age while playing games like *telephone* (GB: *Chinese whispers*).
- Sometimes urban legends do not solely change because of their mostly oral transmission but because a different setting demands minor transformations of the story to fit into the cultural context. This means that differences between various versions of the same urban legend may hint at contrasts in culture. For instance, stories that involve cars are more popular in the United States than in Europe, mainly because cars play a more important role in that culture (Jüngst 1999: 8).

- In fact, most urban legends have their roots in the USA, which has led some people to believe that »... Americans are notoriously concerned more with verisimilitude than with truth. They are gossip-mongers, collectors of scandal, thrivers on rumour, and manifest a childlike belief in any story, no matter how incredible or outrageous, as long as there are enough 'facts' inserted to give it credence« (Brunvand 1988: 15). This account, given by an English journalist, fails to appreciate the fact that urban legends can be found in all regions.
- Several didactic approaches to urban legends have focused on their spooky effect. Reisener (2003: 38), for example, states that they »... combine horror with (black) humour«. While this is certainly true for the stories he selected as examples, it does not account for all urban legends. A look at the index of any anthology of urban legends will show that besides »Creepy Contaminations« or »The Criminal Mind«, there are also categories like »Campus Capers« and »Slapstick Comedy« (Brunvand 1999: 10 ff.). One of the best examples of a funny urban legend is a made-up incident taking place at the coast of Newfoundland (www.snopes .com):

> »ACTUAL transcript of a US naval ship with Canadian authorities off the coast of Newfoundland in October, 1995. This radio conversation was released by the Chief of Naval Operations on 10-10-95.
> Americans: »Please divert your course 15 degrees to the North to avoid a collision.«
> Canadians: »Recommend you divert YOUR course 15 degrees to the South to avoid a collision.«
> Americans: »This is the captain of a US Navy ship. I say again, divert your course.«
> Canadians: »No, I say again, you divert YOUR course.«
> Americans: »This is the aircraft carrier USS Abraham Lincoln, the second largest ship in te United States' Atlantic fleet. We are accompanied by three destroyers, three cruisers and numerous support vessels. I demand that you change your course 15 degrees north. That's one-five degrees north, or counter measures will be undertaken to ensure the safety of this ship.«
> Canadians: »This is a lighthouse. Your call.«

Though being a popular genre of literature, urban legends are still largely underrepresented in the EFL classroom. This may be due to the fact that they are considered nothing more than made up stories, as such being dismissed as unworthy for the classroom. However, they possess qualities that make them very useful in English language education: they are short, plain, exciting, often humorous, easy to understand, containing simple language due to their oral spreading. Hohwiller (2008) has developed a scheme which even proves that urban myths can be used at every stage of learning, as well as help students achieve the various competences connected to TEFL.

Suitable examples can be found in one of the many anthologies written by Brunvand, the largest one being *Too Good to Be True: The Colossal Book of Urban Legends* (1999). Jüngst's book *Urban Legends* (1999) holds a smaller number of urban legends, which have been annotated with German translations for the most difficult words. The most convenient way to find useful stories is over the internet. The most popular source is *snopes.com*, which offers the widest selection of urban legends. Another option is *urbanlegends.about.com*, which is likely to be more appealing to students because of its excessive use of pictures. Though not as systematic as *snopes.com*, it offers in-depth analyses of each urban legend, and contains picture and video hoaxes as well.

2 Procedure

Text	The Clown Statue
Synopsis	A girl babysitting kids is disturbed by a life-sized clown statue in the corner of a room. She phones the kids' father asking him to switch rooms. The father urges her to leave the room immediately because the family has no statue like this. However, the kids have repeatedly complained to be visited by a clown at night but the parents have never taken this seriously assuming it to be a nightmare. The statue turns out to be a man in his clown clothes who hides in the house and goes to the kids' bedrooms at night.
Competences	Reading, speaking, creative writing, text competence
Topics	Horror stories, nightmares, babysitting, children
Level	Intermediate
Time	45' – 90'

Steps (pre – while – post approach):

A. Pre-reading stage
1. T shows a photo (M 1) on a slide and makes S describe it.
2. S are asked to guess the story behind the photo.

B. While-reading stage
1. T plays scary background noises from an electronic device (one of the websites offering free sound files is: www.freesound.org).
2. S read out the story, whose end is missing (M 2, full text: M 3), one after the other (each S one sentence only: class chain).
3. The story is summarized.
4. S tell their experiences with spooky situations.

C. Post-reading stage
1. The genre of urban myths is introduced and characterized via OHP / blackboard / laptop (M 4).
2. S are asked to choose one of three different endings for the story (M 5).
3. (Buffer:) S reconstruct a short, very popular urban legend (M 6). »Squeaky-Canned-Cola« is about a dead mouse in a cola can. The text has been printed on a slide and cut into single sentence snips, which are spread out on the OHP. S come to the front to put the story into the right order.

Homework (three alternatives):
1. Create an urban myth. OR
2. Create an urban myth from four key words (e.g. grandma – oven – granddaughter – emergency). OR
3. Rewrite an urban myth from a new perspective (M 7).

3 Materials

M 1: Photo (http://schermbeck-online.de/wp-con-tent)

M 2: Text without ending (http://urbanlegends.about.com, adapted)

The Clown Statue

A friend of a friend's niece was babysitting for a family in Haunstetten last winter. The family is wealthy and has a very large house – you know the sort, with very many rooms. Anyways, the parents are going to the Augsburg Friedensfest. The father tells the babysitter that once the children are in bed she should go into this specific room and watch TV there because he doesn't want the girl to wander around in the house.

The parents go out and soon she gets the kids into bed and watches TV in the room. Well, she tries watching but she is disturbed by a clown statue in the corner of the room. She tries to ignore it for as long as possible, but it starts freaking her out so much that she can't handle it.

She decides to call the father and asks, »Hey, the kids are in bed, but is it okay if I switch rooms? This clown statue is really creeping me out.«

The father says seriously, »Get the kids, go next door and call 911.«

... How do you think the story will end?

M 3: Text with ending (http://urbanlegends.about.com, adapted)

The Clown Statue

A friend of a friend's niece was babysitting for a family in Haunstetten last winter. The family is wealthy and has a very large house – you know the sort, with very many rooms. Anyways, the parents are going to the Augsburg Friedensfest. The father tells the babysitter that once the children are in bed she should go into this specific room and watch TV there because he doesn't want the girl to wander around in the house.

The parents go out and soon she gets the kids into bed and watches TV in the room. Well, she tries watching but she is disturbed by a clown statue in the corner of the room. She tries to ignore it for as long as possible, but it starts freaking her out so much that she can't handle it.

She decides to call the father and asks, »Hey, the kids are in bed, but is it okay if I switch rooms? This clown statue is really creeping me out.«

The father says seriously, »Get the kids, go next door and call 911.«

She asks, »What's going on?«

He shouts, »Just go next door and once you call the police, call me back.«

She gets the kids, goes next door, and calls the police. When the police are on the way, she calls the father back and asks, »So, really, what's going on?«

He responds, »We don't HAVE a clown statue.« He then further explains that the children have been complaining about a clown watching them as they sleep. He and his wife had just blown it off, assuming that they were having nightmares.

The police arrive and apprehend the »statue«, which turns out to be a man who was dressed as clown and got into the house several weeks ago. He would come into the kids' rooms at nights and watch them while they slept. At daytime he hid into the rooms of the large house.

M 4

Seven Characteristics of Urban Myths

1. They are short.
2. They are often spooky, funny or unbelievable.
3. They are plausible enough to be true.
4. But they are made up in most cases.
5. They are told from one person to another.
6. They often begin with »*A friend of a friend told me...*« or similar expressions.
7. But nobody knows the real author of these stories.

M 5

How does the **Clown Story** end?
On this worksheet you see three possible endings of the story. Give reasons why only one of them is likely to be the end of an urban myth.

1. The father says seriously, »Get the kids, go next door and call 911.«
He explains through the phone that they don't have a clown statue. Instead the kids recently complained about a clown who visits them at night but the parents thought that they have nightmares.
The police arrive and examine the »statue« which turns out to be a man who is dressed as a clown and got into the house several time ago. He came into the kids' rooms at night and watched them sleeping. At daytime he hid into the rooms of the large house.
The moral of this story is to take your children seriously no matter how old they are. The parents from Haunstetten exposed their children to a great danger. Let's hope they have learnt their lesson.

2. The father says seriously, »Get the kids, go next door and call 911.«
The girl asks, »What's going on?«
The father shouts, »Just go next door and once you call the police, call me back.«
She gets the kids, goes next door, and calls the police. When the police are on the way, she calls the father back and asks, »So, really, what's going on?«
He responds, »We don't have a clown statue.« He then further explains that the children have been complaining about a clown watching them as they sleep. He and his wife had just thought that they were having nightmares.
The police arrive and examine the »statue«, which turns out to be a man who was dressed as clown and got into the house several weeks ago. He would come into the kids' rooms at nights and watch them while they slept. At daytime he hid into the rooms of the large house.

3. The father says seriously, »Get the three kids, go next door and call 911.«
She went with the kids into another room where she phoned 991. The police and the parents arrived at the same time. It turned out that the statue is a real man in his clown costume. He hid in one of the rooms and visited the kids' bedroom at night.
Then the father told the girl that the kids said they are visited by a clown at night. He thought that they have bad dreams.

M 6 (Jüngst 1999, 30 f.)

Two friends of a friend are driving at the motorway and stop to have a break at a café besides the road.
They order two cans of cola and drink them besides the car.
As they drink, one of the friends says that his cola tastes a little strange.
However, he thinks no more of it until the last glassful out of the can.
Much to his surprise a dead mouse falls into his glass.
The poor man is taken to hospital and, fortunately, he is alright.
But he sues the cola company and receives several thousand dollars in damages.

M 7 (Jüngst 1999)

The Grocery Fraud
Read the urban myth. Rewrite from the cashier's perspective on about half a page. If you want, write how the story could go on.

A young man is shopping in a supermarket, when he notices that an older woman is staring at him sadly. He moves away but she follows, still staring. And when he finishes shopping, he ends up behind her in a long checkout line. Her grocery basket is full to overflowing; his contains just a few items. She keeps staring at him, sadly making him feel most uncomfortable.
Finally, she speaks up. »You must pardon my staring,« she says, »but you see, you look exactly like my son who died just two weeks ago.«
And she begins to sniffle as she repeats her claim that the young man perfectly resembles her late, beloved son. »I mean exactly like him,« she moans. Then, as the cashier bags her groceries at the front of the line, the woman whispers, »As a favor to a grief-stricken mother, would you mind saying 'Good-bye Mom' to me as I leave? Somehow it would make me feel so much better.«
The young man gulps and agrees to her pathetic request. She gives him a tearful smile, waves, and wheels out her three heavy bags.
»Good-bye, Mom« he says, waving back.
Meanwhile the cashier is ringing up the purchases and finally tells the man that the bill is $ 110.

> »There must be a mistake,« the young man says, pointing at his single small bag.
> »Your mother said you'd be paying for hers, too,« the cashier says.

4 Solutions

A.1. Description of photo
The photo shows a room in a house with sofas, a guitar, and a lamp in the corner. The whole scene is rather dark so it is probably night-time. In one of the corners, you can see a clown statue, which somehow does not fit into the setting of the picture. What also attracts attention is the teenage girl in the foreground, who is only partly visible. She is facing the beholder with a mobile phone to her ear. A speech balloon emerging from the phone reads »Get the kids, go next door and call 911!!!«.
T may add that »911« is the American emergency call – not only the date of the Twin Towers crash(!).

C.2. (M 5)
Text 2 is correct. Text 1 is too moralizing, Text 2 has wrong tenses.

Bibliography
911 surrender (1995). www.snopes.com. (14/08/2015)
Brunvand, Jan (1988). The Mexican Pet: More 'New' Urban Legends and Some Old Favorites. New York/London: Norton.
Brunvand, Jan (1999). Too Good to Be True: The Colossal Book of Urban Legends. New York/London: Norton.
Cloete, Eslie (2007). 'We seek it Here, We Seek it There – That Damn'd Elusive Nandi Bear'. In: Ogude, James/Nyairo, Joyce (eds.) Urban Legends, Colonial Myths: Popular Culture and Literature in East Africa. Trenton: Africa World Press.
Council of Europe (2001). Common European Framework of Reference for Languages: Strasbourg, 30–34.
Emery, David. The Clown Statue. www.aboutentertainment.co.za. (20/08/2015)
Hohwiller, Peter (2008). Urban Legends aus fremdsprachendidaktischer Sicht. Praxis Fremdsprachenunterricht 6:5, 13–17.
Jüngst, Heike (1998). Moderne Großstadtsagen im Englischunterricht für Erwachsene. Neusprachliche Mitteilungen aus Wissenschaft und Praxis 2:51, 95–99.
Jüngst, Heike (1999). Urban Legends. Stuttgart: Reclam.

Reisener, Helmut (2003). Urban Legends – Texts and Tasks. Der Fremdsprachliche Unterricht: Englisch 37:61, 38–42.

Staatsinstitut für Schulqualität und Bildungsforschung München. http://www.
lehrplanplus.bayern.de/fachlehrplan/gymnasium/7/englisch/1-fremdspra-
che. Staatsinstitut für Schulqualität und Bildungsforschung (20/08/2015)

Statue of Limitations. www.snopes. com. (20/08/2015)

Thaler, Engelbert (2008). Teaching English Literature. Paderborn: Schöningh.

Thaler, Engelbert (2015). Kurzprosa im Unterricht. Praxis Fremdsprachenunterricht 1:12, 7–9.

The Babysitter and the Clown Statue (2015). www.urbanlegendsonline.com.
(20/08/2015)

The Obstinate Lighthouse (1995). www.snopes. com. (18/08/2015)

Fables

1 Genre

The fable is a »non-realist« literary genre (Malcom 2012: 66), whose name derives from Latin *fabula*, meaning 'tale'. It is a moral tale which reveals human experiences and depicts conflicts (Detlor 2011: 5). It may illustrate »human foible«, »national embarrassment« or »cultural downfall« (Snodgrass 1998: xiii), but also shows »foolish error«, »social blunder« as well as »personal over-reaching« done by humans (Snodgrass 1998: xv). Because of the moral tag they are equipped with, fables are character builders (Snodgrass 1998: xvi).

The fable shares some characteristics with the allegory, anecdote, parable or folktale, but also has some distinct features. The most outstanding one is its moral tag, which can be put at the beginning or, more often, at the end of the story (Snodgrass 1998: 116; Wimmer 2015). The primary characters of a fable usually are non-human creatures, which can walk, talk and scheme like humans. Additionally, the animals' stereotypic characteristics are depicted, for example the »bloodthirsty wolf« and the »witless sheep« (Snodgrass 1998: 114). Humans also appear as characters, although as »anonymous stock figures« (Snodgrass 1998: 110). The settings are usually simple, such as a deep wood, a hillside or along a stream (Snodgrass 1998: 108). Many fables are not bound by conventions of realism, but depict humans who can change shape, beasts that can talk or witches and wizards who perform magic (Malcom 2012: 66).

Fables are a timeless literary genre. From their first appearance in Babylon as early as 2300 B.C., and Aesop, the »Greek father of Western fable« (Snodgrass 1998: 8), to James Thurber's modern humorous variations: they have entertained and instructed readers and listeners in many cultures. *The Unicorn in the Garden*, which first appeared in The New Yorker in 1939 and is dealt with in this chapter, is probably Thurber's most famous fable.

Fables have also enjoyed a lot of popularity in the classroom. These stories help children to learn, develop, and practice moral reasoning and ethical behaviour. Since they have a clear structure and often rather simple language, they can be used with younger students as well. Additionally, students have to abstract from the specific to the general and must also understand figurative language (Detlor 2011: 4f).

2 Procedure

Text	James Thurber (1940): The Unicorn in the Garden (from: Fables for Our Time and Famous Poems Illustrated. New York: Harper and Brothers)
Synopsis	A husband sees a unicorn in the garden and tells his wife about it. She pokes fun at him, telling him »the unicorn is a mythical beast«, and calls him a »booby« (madman). When he persists, she threatens to send him to a »booby hatch« (insane asylum). After she has summoned the authorities and told them about her husband, they note her own loony-looking face and force her into a straitjacket. They then ask the husband if he told his wife he had seen a unicorn. Not wanting to be locked up himself, he tells them that he has not, because »the unicorn is a mythical beast.« Thus they take the wife away instead, and »the husband lived happily ever after«. The story ends with the »Moral: Don't count your boobies before they're hatched«.
Competences	Listening, reading, speaking, creative writing, text competence, lexical competence
Topics	Outlook on life, peaceful fantasy vs harsh realism, husband vs wife, marital burn-out, fable, parody, fairy tale
Level	Advanced
Time	45–90 minutes

Steps (global-to-deatail approach)

A. Lead-in
1. T shows a picture of a unicorn (M 1) and has S describe it.
2. T gives additional background information: mythical beast, not real.
3. Key lexemes are explained: 'booby' (madman), 'booby-hatch' (insane asylum).

B. First reading / listening
1. T slowly reads out the story up to »'He told me it had a golden horn in the middle of its forehead,' she said.« S just listen.
2. T makes S speculate about the ending.
3. T reads out up to »The husband lived happily ever after.«
4. T asks S to guess the moral.
5. T presents the moral.

C. Global comprehension
S retell the story using the *ball chain technique*: One S starts with the first sentence, and throws a soft ball to a class-mate. This person adds a second sentence and throws the ball to another S, and so on.

D. Second reading
1. T hands out the glossary (M 2).
2. In pairs, S learn the words and test each other.
3. T hands out the text of the fable (M 3).
4. S have to read the text silently.

E. Detailed comprehension
1. S are asked to try and explain the ending, i.e. the husband's victory.
2. The moral is discussed.

F. Analysis
1. To analyse the genre, T presents a grid (M 4), covering the right column.
2. T reads out and explains the features of a fable (left column).
3. In pairs, S are asked to apply these characteristics to the story given.
4. The solutions (right column) are uncovered and discussed.

Homework
Write your own fable (about 150 words) based on one of these morals:
1. Harm set, harm get.
2. A liar will not be believed even when he speaks the truth.
3. Do as you would be done by.

3 Materials

M 1: Picture of unicorn: e.g. Google picture search »unicorn«

M 2: Glossary (alphabetical vocabulary)

English word	English explanation
booby	here: a crazy person
booby-hatch	a place where the insane are kept
breakfast nook	a little side room for eating breakfast
browsing	sampling or tasting here and there
crazy as a jaybird	extremely crazy

cropping	cutting close to the root
cursing	using dirty or obscene speech
gloat	a look of malice or greed
institution	an insane asylum
mythical	relating to a myth, hence not real
psychiatrist	a mental doctor
solemn	grave or serious
strait-jacket	a belted jacket used to confine the violently insane
subdue	capture, seize
unicorn	a mythical beast which looks like a horse with a horn in the center of the head

M 3: Text (http://english.glendale.cc.ca.us/unicorn1.html)

James Thurber: **The Unicorn in the Garden**
Once upon a sunny morning a man who sat in a breakfast nook looked up from his scrambled eggs to see a white unicorn with a golden horn quietly cropping the roses in the garden. The man went up to the bedroom where his wife was still asleep and woke her. »There's a unicorn in the garden,« he said. »Eating roses.« She opened one unfriendly eye and looked at him. »The unicorn is a mythical beast,« she said, and turned her back on him. The man walked slowly downstairs and out into the garden. The unicorn was still there; now he was browsing among the tulips. »Here, unicorn,« said the man, and he pulled up a lily and gave it to him. The unicorn ate it gravely. With a high heart, because there was a unicorn in his garden, the man went upstairs and roused his wife again. »The unicorn,« he said, »ate a lily.« His wife sat up in bed and looked at him coldly. »You are a booby,« she said, »and I am going to have you put in the booby-hatch.«
The man, who had never liked the words »booby« and »booby-hatch«, and who liked them even less on a shining morning when there was a unicorn in the garden, thought for a moment. »We'll see about that,« he said. He walked over to the door. »He has a golden horn in the middle of his forehead,« he told her. Then he went back to the garden to watch the unicorn; but the unicorn had gone away. The man sat down among the roses and went to sleep.

As soon as the husband had gone out of the house, the wife got up and dressed as fast as she could. She was very excited and there was a gloat in her eye. She telephoned the police and she telephoned a psychiatrist; she told them to hurry to her house and bring a strait-jacket. When the police and the psychiatrist arrived they sat down in chairs and looked at her, with great interest.

»My husband,« she said, »saw a unicorn this morning.« The police looked at the psychiatrist and the psychiatrist looked at the police. »He told me it ate a lilly,« she said. The psychiatrist looked at the police and the police looked at the psychiatrist. »He told me it had a golden horn in the middle of its forehead,« she said. At a solemn signal from the psychiatrist, the police leaped from their chairs and seized the wife. They had a hard time subduing her, for she put up a terrific struggle, but they finally subdued her. Just as they got her into the strait-jacket, the husband came back into the house.

»Did you tell your wife you saw a unicorn?« asked the police. »Of course not,« said the husband. »The unicorn is a mythical beast.« »That's all I wanted to know,« said the psychiatrist. »Take her away. I'm sorry, sir, but your wife is as crazy as a jaybird.«

So they took her away, cursing and screaming, and shut her up in an institution. The husband lived happily ever after.

Moral: Don't count your boobies until they are hatched.

M 4: Genre analysis (transparency, slide, board sketch)

Characteristics of fable	The Unicorn in the Garden
short in length	530 words
ending: »moral«	- »Moral: Don't count … hatched.« - fairy tale ending: »the husband lived happily ever after«
Three-part structure: 1. introduction 2. conflict 3. moral	1. husband sees unicorn 2. husband vs wife 3. Don't count your boobies …
often only two characters	husband, wife (and unicorn)
animals representing humans	no anthropomorphic animals as characters, only unicorn ▸ focus on humans' reactions

human characteristics criticized	Aggressiveness and belligerence, lack of intellectual and emotional empathy, negation of fantasy
past tense	past tense
▼ fable & fairy tale & parody	

4 Solutions

E.1. Ending
husband's victory:
- struggle between husband and wife ▶
- peaceful fantasy vs. harsh realism
- victory achieved by role reversal: husband stakes claim to realism after wife ironically repeats husband's fantastic claims

E.2. Moral
»Don't count your boobies until they are hatched«:
- word-play on the popular American adage »Don't count your chickens (babies) before they are hatched«
- meaning: don't count on things to turn out exactly as you planned them

Bibliography
Detlor, Theda (2011). Teaching with Aesop's Fables. New York: Scholastic Inc.
Malcom, David (2012). British and Irish Short Story Handbook. Blackwell Literature Handbooks. Malden: Wiles-Blackwell.
Snodgrass, Mary Ellen (1998). Encyclopedia of Fable. Santa Barbara: ABC-CLIO.
Wimmer, Joshua (2015). Fable in Literature. Definition & Examples. http://study.com/academy/lesson/fable-in-literature-definition-examples.html. (23/08/2015)

Fairy Tale (Parody)

1 Genre

»If you want your children to be intelligent, read them fairy tales. If you want them to be more intelligent, read them more fairy tales.« Albert Einstein's conviction rephrases what the Brothers Grimm pointed out about the pedagogic significance of fairy tales in the first half of the 19th century (Geister 2010; Winick 2013). The morals and virtues communicated within fairy tales may help foster children's education and the formation of their personality – despite the controversial discussions on their value in later decades.

Fairy tales or folk tales are short fictional narratives which are mostly anonymously authored and collectively owned (e.g. Jones 2002). They are classified as a sub-genre of folk narrative. A first distinction is usually made between genuine folk tales (*Volksmärchen*), which have a long oral tradition, and literary or »arty« fairy tales (*Kunstmärchen*), which are written by single authors. The first are characterized by the simple language of common people (sometimes even including dialect), a linear narrative, and a narrative situation that is often adapted by the storyteller. As the latter are individual creations, their plot and style are often more complex (e.g. Hans Christian Andersen, Wilhelm Hauff). The Grimm Brothers' collection of »Children's and Household Tales«, which comprises 200 fairy tales (plus 28 stories in the appendix), is usually considered as an anthology of folk tales, as the authors wrote them down based on the narratives of the folk (Michaelis-Jena 1971; Uther 2013).

The typical features of fairy tales are the following:
- a supernatural, miraculous element
- one-dimensional delineation of plot, setting, characters
- recurrent characters (stepmothers, princesses) and motifs (keys, apples, mirrors, rings and toads)
- difficulties which have to be overcome
- repetitions
- formulaic phrases (Once upon a time … and they lived happily hereafter)
- numbers like three, seven, twelve or 100
- happy endings expressing hope

Haase (2008: 323) specifies three basic elements of fairy tales: (1) The structure is episodic and constructed primarily on motifs; (2) the genre is fictional, the setting indefinite, and the mode of reality supernatural or fantastic; (3) the protagonists overcome obstacles to advance to rewards and a new level of existence.

Parodies have been a precious contribution to English literature and culture from the beginning of the 14th century (Geoffrey Chaucer's Canterbury Tales) up to today's popular Disney fairy tales like Shrek or Tangled (Kullmann 2008: 138; Ranke 2008: 578; Thaler 2008: 79). A parody is »a work that imitates another work in order to ridicule the work, its subject or author« (Thaler 2008: 79), usually by maintaining its form but changing the content (Ranke 2008: 577), e.g. via plot twists or satirical elements.

Fairy tale parodies are usually based on a common folktale from oral tradition, which is rewritten to evoke humour. Typical fairy tale motifs like magic, princesses and princes, archaic language, improbable plot, and repetitive structure can become the targets of intertextual mockery (Eisfeld 2014; Kullmann 2008: 132f.; Ranke 2008: 580). To make the original plot head into a different direction, various ploys can be employed: changing characters into animals, choosing another character (maybe the evil one) as the protagonist, inventing new characters, including characters from other fairy tales, changing their personality traits, making use of reverse gender roles, altering the setting, elaborating on the ending, or transforming the text type, e.g. rewriting the original plot into a rap song, a poem, a play, or a newspaper article with quotes from central characters.

2 Procedure

Text	James Thurber: The Princess and the Tin Box (The New Yorker, September 29, 1945)
Synopsis	The princess, who is used to precious jewels, reaches the age of eighteen. Her father, the king, announces to the courts of five neighboring kingdoms that he will give his daughter in marriage to the prince who brings her the gift she likes most. Three of the princes offer expensive decorative gifts, and the last, who is poor yet handsome, brings a tin box with non-precious metal in it. Although she is amused by the latter gift, she eventually chooses the jewel box and marries the prince who brought that.

Competences	Reading, speaking, argumentative (or creative) writing, text competence, language awareness
Topics	Money, youth, marriage, relationships, materialism, idealism, reader expectations, fairy tales, parodies, fables
Level	Upper-intermediate to advanced
Time:	90 minutes

Steps (pre – while – post reading):

A. Pre-reading stage
1. T writes the title and the first words (»Once upon a time«) of the story on the board.
2. S are asked to speculate about the genre and plot of the story.

B. While-reading stage
1. T hands out the text of the story (M 1).
2. T reads out the story slowly up to »... the king said to his daughter, 'you must select the gift you like best and marry the prince that brought it.'«
3. S have to guess who the princess will marry.
4. T reads the rest.
5. Ending and moral are discussed.

C. Post-reading stage
1. Genre:
a) The whole class collects typical features of a fairy tale present in this story. The results are collected on the board (transparency ...).
b) T: »In pairs, scan the text for elements that prove that this is a »funny fairy tale«, i.e. an ironic treatment of this genre.«
2. Alternatives:
a) »In groups of three, create an alternative ending and moral.«
b) The S's suggestions are collected and discussed.
c) T presents five humorous alternatives for ending and moral (M 2). One after the other ending is disclosed, with the moral covered each time. S are asked to guess the respective moral.

Homework (2 options)
1. Individually: Write a comment of about 100 words on Oscar Wilde's famous aphorism: »When I was young, I thought that money was the most important thing in life; now that I'm old I know that it is.« OR
2. Group of three: Invent your own fairy tale parody. The worksheet (M 3) will give you some ideas.

3 Materials

M 1: Text (http://shortstories.co.in/the-princess-and-the-tin-box/)

The Princess and the Tin Box

Once upon a time, in a far country, there lived a king whose daughter was the prettiest princess in the world. Her eyes were like the cornflower, her hair was sweeter than the hyacinth, and her throat made the swan look dusty.

From the time she was a year old, the princess had been showered with presents. Her nursery looked like Cartier's window. Her toys were all made of gold or platinum or diamonds or emeralds. She was not permitted to have wooden blocks or china dolls or rubber dogs or linen books, because such materials were considered cheap for the daughter of a king.

When she was seven, she was allowed to attend the wedding of her brother and throw real pearls at the bride instead of rice. Only the nightingale, with his lyre of gold, was permitted to sing for the princess. The common blackbird, with his boxwood flute, was kept out of the palace grounds. She walked in silver-and-samite slippers to a sapphire-and-topaz bathroom and slept in an ivory bed inlaid with rubies.

On the day the princess was eighteen, the king sent a royal ambassador to the courts of five neighboring kingdoms to announce that he would give his daughter's hand in marriage to the prince who brought her the gift she liked the most.

The first prince to arrive at the palace rode a swift white stallion and laid at the feet of the princess an enormous apple made of solid gold which he had taken from a dragon who had guarded it for a thousand years. It was placed on a long ebony table set up to hold the gifts of the princess's suitors. The second prince, who came on a gray charger, brought her a nightingale made of a thousand diamonds, and it was placed beside the golden apple. The third prince, riding on a black horse, carried a great jewel box made of platinum and sapphires, and it was placed next to the diamond nightingale. The fourth prince, astride a fiery yellow horse, gave the princess a gigantic heart made of rubies and pierced by an emerald arrow. It was placed next to the platinum-and-sapphire jewel box.

Now the fifth prince was the strongest and handsomest of all the five suitors, but he was the son of a poor king whose realm had been overrun by mice and locusts and wizards and mining engineers so that there was nothing much of value left in it. He came plodding up to the palace of the princess on a plow horse and he brought her a small tin box filled with mica and feldspar and hornblende which he had picked up on the way.

The other princes roared with disdainful laughter when they saw the tawdry gift the fifth prince had brought to the princess. But she examined it with great interest and squealed with delight, for all her life she had never seen tin before or mica or feldspar or hornblende. The tin box was placed next to the ruby heart pierced with an emerald arrow.

»Now,« the king said to his daughter, »you must select the gift you like best and marry the prince that brought it.«

The princess smiled and walked up to the table and picked up the present she liked the most. It was the platinum-and-sapphire jewel box, the gift of the third prince.

»The way I figure it,« she said, »is this. It is a very large and expensive box, and when I am married, I will meet many admirers who will give me precious gems with which to fill it to the top. Therefore, it is the most valuable of all the gifts my suitors have brought me and I like it the best.«

The princess married the third prince that very day in the midst of great merriment and high revelry. More than a hundred thousand pearls were thrown at her, and she loved it.

Moral: *All those who thought the princess was going to select the tin box filled with worthless stones instead of one of the other gifts will kindly stay after class and write one hundred times on the blackboard »I would rather have a hunk of aluminum silicate than a diamond necklace.«*

Annotations: *nursery* – child's playroom; *stallion* – male horse; *suitor* – man wishing to marry a woman; *charger* – horse used in battles; *locust* – insect that destroys crops; *wizard* – man with magical powers; *to plod* – to move slowly and heavily; *mica / feldspar / hornblende* – colourful, but worthless stones; *tawdry* – lacking good taste; *to glut with* – to give too much of; *gem* – precious stone; *revelry* – dancing, singing and feasting.

M 2: Alternative endings & morals (Burghardt/Stevenson 1983)

Alternative endings	Alternative morals
1. The princess marries the poor prince, saying »Everybody knows this is the way to get even richer«.	Even princesses read fairy tales.
2. She marries one of the rich princes, divorces him, demands alimony, runs off with the poor but handsome prince, and lives happily ever after.	What's yours is mine, and what's mine is my own.
3. She marries the poor prince, but he turns out to be a drug addict / gambler / wife-beater.	Happy endings have gone out of fashion.
4. She marries the poor prince, starts a terrorist campaign against mice, locusts and mining engineers, and has the time of her life.	Ulrike Meinhof, eat your heart out!
5. She marries the poor prince, invests some of her riches in his impoverished kingdom, turns it into an industrial zone or tourist attraction, and gets even richer than she was before.	Judicious capital investment can pay dividends.

M 3: Ideas for fairy tale parody

Parody Planner
Use the following suggestions to plan your story. Take the right column for your ideas. You do not need to write full sentences.

1. Original fairy tale	
Decide on a specific tale you want to parody. ▶ Snow White, Little Red Riding Hood ...	
2. Characters	
Who are your characters? Give them names and brief descriptions. ▶ add a character from another tale, change roles, change the hero into an anti-hero, invent a new character, turn it into an animal ...	

3. Setting	
Where and when does your story take place? ▸ in medieval forests? 19th century Wild West? Modern-day New York? Other planet in the future? ...	
4. Plot	
What is the story-line / conflict / climax? ▸ ridicule the magical elements, exaggerate the fights, extend the ending (What happened after the marriage?) ...	
5. Conclusion	
How does the tale end? ▸ a funny or sad ending? Will they live happily ever after?	
6. Language	
What typical phrases are used? ▸ re-write them, turn them into the opposite, »Fridge, oh fridge, next to the wall! Who is the ugliest of them all?«	

4 Solutions

B.3. Guesses: probably poor prince because:
- Money isn't everything.
- All that glitters isn't gold.
- Money can't buy me love.

B.5.
- ending: In fairy tales, the princess invariably falls for the prince with the purest heart (and the most handsome looks). However, in this story, that idealized notion is tossed aside for a more mercenary choice.
- moral: a) materialism triumphs over idealism (cynical moral) b) reproach to the naïve reader

C.1.: Board sketch (slide/transparency)

Classic fairy tale
- Beginning/ending: opening (and closing) formulae (»Once upon a time«)
- Characters: princess, king, princes
- Situation: princess has to choose one of the princes
- Setting: far away country in the past
- Language: archaic, romantic comparisons with flowers and swans
- Structure: repetitive sequence of events

»Funny fairy tale« (genre mixture)
- elements of parody: cynical moral, anachronistic references (»Cartier's window«, »mining engineers«), exaggerations (five instead of three princes, overdoing the archaic style, exaggerated alliterations: »plodding up to the palace of the princess on a plow horse«)
- elements of fable: explicit moral, though no animals as protagonists

Bibliography
Burghardt, Klaus/Stevenson, Douglas (1983). Twelve Short Masterpieces. Stuttgart: Klett.
Eisfeld, Conny (2014). How Fairy Tales Live Happily ever after. The Art of Adapting Fairy Tales. Hamburg: Anchor Academic Publishing.
Geister, Oliver (2010). Kleine Pädagogik des Märchens. Begriff – Geschichte – Ideen für Erziehung und Unterricht. Baltmannsweiler: Schneider.
Haase, Donald. Fairy Tales (2008). In: Haase, Donald (ed.) Greenwood Encyclopedia of Folktales and Fairy Tales, Vol. 1. Westport: Greenwood Press.
Jones, Swann (2002). The Fairy Tale. New York: Routledge.
Kullmann, Thomas (2008). Englische Kinder- und Jugendliteratur – eine Einführung. Grundlagen der Anglistik und Amerikanistik 31, 132–138.
Michaelis-Jena, Ruth (1971). Oral Tradition and the Brothers Grimm. In: Folklore 82:4, 265–275. URL: http://www.jstor.org/stable/1260545. (15/08/2015)
Ranke, Kurt (2008). Parodie. Enzyklopädie des Märchens: Nibelungenlied – Prozeßmotive 10, 577–583.
Thaler, Engelbert (2008). Teaching English Literature. Paderborn: Schöningh.
Thompson, Stith (1977). The Folktale. Berkeley: University of California Press.
Uther, Hans-Jörg (2013). Handbuch zu den Kinder- und Hausmärchen der Brüder Grimm: Entstehung – Wirkung – Interpretation. Göttingen: De Gruyter.
Winick, Stephan (2013). Einstein's Folklore. http://blogs.loc.gov/folklife/2013/12/einsteins-folklore/. (11/08/15)

Jokes

1 Genre

»A joke is a short humorous piece of oral literature in which the funniness culminates in the final sentence, called the punchline« (Hetzron 1991: 65 f.). This punchline is intended to make the audience laugh. By using logical incompatibility, nonsense, puns, homophones or other means, it makes the listeners (or readers) aware that the story contains a second, conflicting meaning. The tension reaches its highest level at the very end, and no further words should be added to relieve the tension.

A good joke is succinct, contains no more detail than needed to set the scene for the punchline, takes the set-up of the audience into consideration, and respects the cultural context (Watkins 2007).

As it is basically an oral tradition, telling a joke is a cooperative effort. Referring to conversation analysis, Sacks (1974) distinguishes between three serially ordered types of sequences: the preface/framing (»Did you hear about this one?«), the telling, and the audience's response.

2 Procedure

Text	Collection of various jokes
Competences	(Declarative and procedural) grammatical competence, reading, speaking
Topics	Humour, grammar, tenses
Level	From lower intermediate
Time	45 minutes

Steps:
1. Lead-in
T tells a joke of his choice.

2. Individual work
The worksheet (M 1) with jokes containing mixed tenses is handed out. S are asked to fill in the correct tenses.

3. Group work
T first shows a slide with the four tasks for the working phase:
a) Discuss which tense should be used in your joke and why.
b) Explain the main point of the joke.
c) Decide if the tense has any relevance for the meaning of the joke.
d) Do you like the joke? Why/Why not?
Then S get together in groups of three. Internally they have to decide on one group presenter. Each group gets one joke.

4. Presentation
The results are presented by the group speakers. Mistakes are corrected. Conflicting opinions are discussed.

5. Homework
Each student has to prepare a joke containing a certain tense, which has to be presented the following lesson.

3 Materials

M 1 (Thaler 2012)

Jokes: Mixed Tenses

1. Officer: Get out of the lake; there's no bathing allowed here!
Ian: I .... (not to bathe). I .... (to drown)!
2. Teacher: Today, we're going to talk about the tenses. Now, if
I .... (to say) »I am beautiful«, which tense .... (to be) it?
Student: Obviously it is the past tense.
3. Teacher: .... (to name) two days of the week
that .... (to start) with the letter 't'.
Pupil: Today and tomorrow.
4. An adult is someone who .... (to cease) to grow vertically but
not horizontally.
5. Dentist: Stop screaming, boy. I .... (to touch, even) your
tooth. In fact you're not even in the chair yet.
Peter: I know. But you .... (to stand) on my foot for ten
minutes.
6. Robert: .... (you, to hear) about the Scot who .... (to
win) a holiday for two in Majorca? He .... (to go) by himself twice.
7 John: I .... (to eat) beef all my life and now I'm
strong as an ox.
Sam: That's funny. I .... (to eat) fish all my life and I can't
swim a stroke.
8. Patient: Doctor! Doctor! I .... (just, to swallow)
seven snooker balls – four reds, a brown, a pink and a black. I feel terrible!
Doctor: I know what the problem is. You .... (not to eat)
your greens.

---

4 Solutions

M 1
1. I'm not bathing, I'm drowning
2. say, is
3. Name, start
4. ceases/has ceased

5. haven't even touched, have been standing
6. Did you hear/have you heard, won, went
7. have been eating, have been eating
8. have just swallowed, haven't eaten

Bibliography
Hetzron, Robert (1991). On the Structure of Punchlines. Humor: International
   Journal of Humor Research 4(1), 61–108.
Sacks, Harvey (1974). An Analysis of the Course of a Joke's Telling in Conver-
   sation. In: Bauman, Richard/Sherzer, Joel. Explorations in the Ethnography of
   Speaking. Cambridge: Cambridge University Press, 337–353.
Thaler, Engelbert (2012). 10 Modern Approaches to Teaching Grammar. Pader-
   born: Schöningh.
Watkins, Carol (2007). What makes a Good Joke? http://ncpamd.com/fair-hu-
   mor/. (10/08/2015)

Mini-sagas

1 Genre

»A mini-saga is kind of a summary but there are certain rules. You have to tell a story in fifty words. Not ninety-nine and not fifty-one but exactly fifty. This might sound easy but it is not as easy as it sounds. You think this is a mini-saga?« (Thaler 2009: 53). According to this meta-mini-saga, i.e. a mini-saga describing the features of a mini-saga, this genre consists of exactly 50 words – plus a title with up to 15 extra signs.

Invented by the British science-fiction author Brian Aldiss in the early 1980s, the first mini-saga was printed in *The Sunday Telegraph* in 1982 after a competition was held asking readers to write a short story in exactly 50 words. These words are usually structured into introduction (usually the first sentence) – main part – end, often with an abrupt beginning and an open or unexpected end.

Another form of micro-fiction is *55 Fiction*, which is basically the same as the mini-saga but with 55 instead of 50 words. Its origin dates back to 1987, when a writing contest was organized by the New Times (California). This newspaper, among several others, still runs a competition, and anybody, including school students, can submit their own 55 fiction (Moss 2015).

A second variation is called *drabbles*, consisting of 100 words in length, with the title not necessarily included. This format was introduced by the Birmingham University Science Fiction Society, who took the term *drabble* from Monty Python's *Big Red Book* (1971), in which *drabble* is described as a word game where the first participant to write a novel is the winner. Like for 50- or 55-word fiction, there are numerous drabble contests all over the world (Smith 2015; Meades/Wake 1988, 1990; Howe/Wake 1993).

As mini-sagas are often written in a simple, easy-to-read style, even students with lower language proficiency can fairly well understand them. Reading for information and for pleasure can be combined because they often reveal interesting insights in a humorous way. Due to the extreme brevity of the genre, the task to write a mini-saga (or 55 fiction, or drabble) forces students to express meaningful ideas in a limited space precisely, focusing on both storyline and specific language items, and concentrating on the bare essentials of a story (vgl. z. B. Siebold 2015).

2 Procedure

Texts	1. Tiny Girl 2. Friends at the End
Synopsis	1. *Tiny Girl:* A girl who is bullied by her classmates eventually commits suicide on the school campus. 2. *Friends at the End* The two friends Frank and Dave have a meaningful conversation. At the end it turns out that Dave is a prison officer on the death row and accompanies his very good friend Frank on his way to execution.
Competences	Reading, speaking, text competence, intercultural communicative competence, creative writing
Topics	Social relations, sad ending, death, capital punishment, friendship, mini-sagas and drabbles
Level	Intermediate to advanced
Time	45 minutes

Steps:

A. Pre-reading
1. T writes the titles of the two texts on the board.
2. S get together in pairs (A and B).
3. In pairs, A students speculate about the plot of title 1, B students about the plot of title 2.
4. A few guesses are collected in class.

B. While-reading
1. A students get text 1 (M 1), B students text 2 (M 2).
2. The stories are read silently.
3. The two partners retell each other their stories.
4. They exchange their opinions on the two stories.

C. Post-reading
1. T asks S to count the number of words (without heading, contractions counted as one word).
2. The genres of mini-saga and drabble are described and compared.
3. Similarities and differences between the two stories are discussed.

Homework (*Creative writing*)
1. Write an alternative – maybe more humorous – ending of your story consisting of 50 (100) words.
2. Write a mini-saga (or drabble) on the antonym of death, i.e. birth.

3 Materials

M 1: Text 1 (Thaler 2009: 53)

Tiny Girl
Lisa was 1.35 meters small. The kids in her class laughed at her and said »Tiny girl never grows«. She was sad but also angry and so she climbed up onto the roof in the big break and shouted »Now I am bigger than you«. Then she jumped and died.

M 2: Text 2 (Mott 2014: 6)

Friends at the End
With his meal finished, Fred belched contentedly.
Dave leaned in the doorway, »Fred, are you ready? It's time to go.«
Briefly scanning his surroundings, Fred gave quick nod and followed Dave out the door.
Dave halted abruptly and turned. »Fred, I've known you for 20 years now, and I didn't want this, but it's out of my hands.«
»Thanks Dave. That really means a lot, and I don't blame you at all.«
»I appreciate that, Fred.«
Wiping tears from his eyes, Fred choked, »We'll meet again, Dave.«
Exhaling deeply to compose himself, Dave faced forward and announced »Dead man walking!«

4 Solutions

C.2.
- Mini-saga/minisaga/mini saga (text 1): a short piece of writing containing exactly 50 words, plus a title of up to 15 signs
- drabble (text 2): a short work of fiction of one hundred words in length, not necessarily including the title

C 3.
- similarities: sad ending, death, human relationships, surprising resolution in last sentence ...
- differences: suicide vs capital punishment, bullying vs friendship, cultural context ...

Bibliography
Howe, David/Wake, David (eds.) (1993). Drabble Who. Harold Wood: Beccon Publications.
Meades, Rob/Wake, David (eds.) (1988). The Drabble Project. Harold Wood: Beccon Publications.
Meades, Rob/Wake, David (eds.) (1990). Drabble II: Double Century. Harold Wood: Beccon Publications.
Moss, Steve (2015). Special Issue – 55 Fiction. http://www.newtimesslo.com/special-issue/8/55-fiction/how-to-enter/ (03/08/2015)
Mott, Jason (2014). Here a Drabble, There a Drabble. E-book. Smashwords: Mott.
Siebold, Jörg (2015). Jedes Wort zählt! Und noch einmal Minisagas. Praxis Fremdsprachenunterricht. Basisheft 1:15, 4–8.
Smith, Liz (2011). Laurier Launches Literary Competition to Commemorate Centennial Year. The Cord Weekly. http://www.thecord.ca/ (03/08/2015)
Thaler, Engelbert (2008). Teaching English Literature. Paderborn: Schöningh.
Thaler, Engelbert (2009). Method Guide: Kreative Methoden für den Literaturunterricht in den Klassen 7–12. Paderborn: Schöningh.

Nasreddin

1 Genre

Usually portrayed with a turban and riding on a donkey, Nasreddin is a witty and intelligent person, who is down to earth and has no prejudices against others. »Wit, common sense, ingenuousness, ridicule … and the kind of humour that reflects human psychology, exposes the shortcomings of a society, criticizes even state and religious affairs yet always settles matters amicably are the elements which together create a special kind of logic, the Nasreddin Hodja logic« (Schiff 2015: 1). These features lend Hodja stories a certain immortal appeal.

The protagonist of these very short stories may – or may not – have lived somewhere in the Middle East in the 13th century. The stories were spread orally in the Muslim world and later translated into many different languages, enjoying popularity from the Mediterranean Sea to China (Javadi 2009). »The themes often have a universal appeal and are frequently very widely distributed across cultures, so they make ideal reading in the early stages of the language-learning process« (Baynham 1986: 133 f.).

Nasreddin stories are brief tales centred on episodes and incidents in the (fictional or real) life of the Sufi scholar Nasreddin. Usually described as a wise and learned person, Nasreddin is considered an expert in religion and law (Kanik 1982: 3 ff.). At first glance, Nasreddin acts in an unconventional and absurd way, his behaviour seeming odd, impudent and illogical. Yet, it gradually becomes clear that Nasreddin's actions and statements are extremely clever, witty, and even philosophical. Combining wisdom with unconventionality and humour, Nasreddin may be labelled a trickster character (Javadi 2009; Thaler 2008: 82). The trickster, a popular character in literature (cf. Till Eulenspiegel, the Nordic god Loki), plays tricks on other people, in particular the powerful and arrogant. Nasreddin may be regarded as a well-educated Eulenspiegel in an eastern setting.

2 Procedure

Text	The Sermon – a Nasreddin Story (Eskicioglu 2015)
Synopsis	The Sufi scholar Nasreddin is appointed the new Imam of the village. His responsibilities include giving a sermon at the local mosque each day. Nasreddin, however, is unwilling to fulfil his task and attempts to rid himself of this inconvenient duty. By asking clever questions he tricks the congregation three days in a row and manages to accomplish his goal. Thus he is able to leave the mosque each day without having to deliver the long anticipated sermon.
Competences	Listening, speaking, reading, acting, text competence, researching
Topics	Nasreddin, trickster tales and characters, effective writing, the power of words
Level	Intermediate
Time	45 minutes (or 90' if acting is part of the lesson)

Steps:

A. Pre-listening
1. T has class describe the man in the picture (M 1).
2. Individually, S speculate about Nasreddin's character traits by writing down three adjectives or nouns.

B. While-listening
1. T reads out the first three paragraphs (without the last one).
2. The story is summarized in the form of a class chain: each S says one sentence.
3. S are asked to compare their expectations about Nasreddin's personality with the information they have received about him so far in the story.
4. Impulse: How would you feel if you were part of the congregation?

C. Post-listening
1. S create the ending themselves. They get together in groups of four and have two alternative tasks, one for each pair:
- Task a) What will happen on the third day? Write an ending in which Nasreddin is able to avoid the sermon another time.
- Task b) What will happen on the third day? Imagine that Nasreddin asks the congregation again whether they know what he is about to tell them today. How will the people be able to make sure that they finally get a sermon?
2. After writing, the group decides on the best ending.
3. In their group, S prepate a short play based on the ending they have chosen.
4. S present the play to the class.

D. Conclusion
1. Teacher reveals the original ending (M 2).
2. S compare the ending with their own alternatives.
3. The meaning of the original is discussed.

Homework
S have to find another Nasreddin story (in the Internet), which they like, and bring it to class the following lesson.

3 Materials

M 1: Picture of Nasreddin (Alioğlu 2014)

M 2: Full text (Eskicioglu 2015)

The Sermon

On his first day as the village's imam, Nasreddin Hodja was seated on the raised bench, preparing to give his sermon. The congregation was quite anxious to hear what he had to say. But the Hodja didn't really have a sermon ready.

»Do you know what I am about to tell you today?« he asked. »No, Hodja Effendi, we don't.« they replied. »If you don't know what I am going to talk about,« the Hodja said, »then I have nothing to tell you.« And with that, he got up and left the mosque, leaving the puzzled people behind him.

The next day, when it was the time of the sermon, Hodja was back on his seat and the congregation curiously waiting. »Do you know what I am about to tell you today?« Hodja asked again. Having learned from the previous day, the people did not want to say »no« this time. »Yes, Hodja Effendi,« they all shouted, »we know.« »Well,« said the Hodja, »if you already know what I am going to tell you, then I don't need to tell it to you!« He got up and left. The people gathered in the mosque were at a loss.

The third day Hodja came and sat down, and asked his question. »Do you know what I am about to tell you today?« The congregation was not going to let Hodja get away this time without giving a sermon. Some of them replied with »yes, we do« and some of them replied with »no, we don't.« »In that case,« said the Hodja, »Those who do know should tell the ones who do not know« and slipped out of the mosque.

---

4 Solutions

D.3. Interpretation

In general, analysing Nasreddin stories is a challenge. From a moral standpoint, the scholar's behaviour in the tale has to be condemned since his main motivation may be identified as pure laziness. Nasreddin is just not willing to fulfil his duty and uses his cunning intelligence to avoid delivering the disagreeable sermon.

Moreover Nasreddin does not find himself in a position in which he could justify his behaviour by pointing to unfair treatment. Actually, the village has chosen him as their new Imam entrusting him with a highly honourable task.

Bluntly spoken, by refusing to give a sermon he betrays his own community's confidence and respect.

Or is there a deeper meaning between the lines? Intelligence and rhetorics are powerful instruments. What you need to reach your aims is brain and words. If you are cunning and eloquent, it is even possible to trick other people and neglect your duty. Is it also legitimate? The fact that Nasreddin gets away scot-free may lead to that reading.

Of course this kind of interpretation is somewhat problematic, especially in a classroom context. So the discussion about Nasreddin's behaviour should also question Nasreddin's status of a role model.

Bibliography
Alioğlu, Sait (2014). »Nasreddin Hoca, Ahi Evren midir«. www.kitaphaber.com. tr/nasreddin-hoca-ahi-evren-midir-k1645.html. (27/08/15)
Eskicioglu, Lale. Who is Nasreddin Hodja. http://www.readliterature.com /hodjastories.htm. (28/08/2015)
Javadi, Hasan (2009). Molla Nasreddin. In: Encyclopedia Iranica. http://www.iranica online.org/ articles/molla-nasreddin-i-the-person. (28/08/2015)
Kanik, Orhan (1982). Das Wort des Esels. Geschichten von Nasreddin Hodscha. Berlin: Ararat Verlag.
Schiff, Jeremy (2015). Nasreddin Hodja. http://u.cs.biu.ac.il/~schiff/Net/front. html#intro. (23/08/15)
Thaler, Engelbert (2008). Teaching English Literature. München: Schöningh.

Picture Books

1 Genre

The general term *picture book* refers to a piece of literature containing both text and illustrations (Enever 2006; Nespeca/Reeve 2003). Bader (1976: 1) offers a more detailed definition, emphasizing the value of picture books as objects of cultural value for children: »A picturebook is text, illustrations, total design; an item of manufacture and a commercial product; a social, cultural, historic document; and foremost, an experience for a child. As an art form it hinges on the interdependence of pictures and words, on the simultaneous display of two facing pages, and on the drama of the turning page.«

Concerning the formal specifications, the aspect of brevity is respected in most picture books. Usually they contain fewer than 500 words on an average page count of 32 pages (Peterson/Swartz 2008).

Depending on the relationship between the plot and its illustrations, a variety of subtypes can be classified (Silvey 1995):

- The *pure* or *true picture book* contains no or very little text. Counting books or alphabet books are the most prominent examples of this genre.
- In the *wordless book* the whole plot is only told by the illustrations. The absence of any textual element therefore has to be compensated by rich visuals.
- In *picture storybooks*, the text is complemented by illustrations, which have a supportive function and often mirror the plot, but the plot itself is told by the text. The example which will be presented in the following (*It's a Book* by Lane Smith) is part of this category. Another well-known example is *The Gruffalo*.
- The *illustrated book* contains more text than pictures. However, the text is often kept in a simple way, since the target group of these books is beginning readers. The illustrations often serve to facilitate comprehension, but sometimes they are only ornamental and non-functional.
- The last subgenre is a rather new type of picture books: *Toy* and *movable books* do not only offer text and illustrations, but these two integral elements are accompanied by haptic elements or pop-up-illustrations.

2 Procedure

Text	Lane Smith: *It's a Book*
Synopsis	This wonderful 32-page picture book is a delightful manifesto on behalf of print in the digital age. A mouse, a jackass and a monkey discover a new thing – a book! Flat and rectangular, with a hard cover and a soft inside, it bewilders the jackass, while the monkey patiently tries to explain its curious technology. »Do you blog with it?« the jackass asks. »No, it's a book,« the monkey replies, and this only makes the donkey's irritation bigger: »Where's the mouse? Does it need a password? Can it text, tweet, toot?« »No, none of that«, the monkey explains ...
Competences	Listening, lexical competence, speaking, acting
Topics	Books, digital devices, entertainment, readerly happiness (*flow feeling*)
Level	From beginners
Time	45 minutes

Steps:

A. Lead-in
1. S are asked to take cinema seat position.
2. T shows the cover of the book he has brought along.
3. S guess on the title.

B. Vocabulary
1. Presentation: T uses picture cards to explain the meaning of unknown words (M 1): *to scroll, to blog, to tweet, Wi-Fi, letter, to fix, screen, library, to charge.*
2. Consolidation: T announces that they will play Bingo with the new words. Every S gets a Bingo sheet (M 2). When T reads out a new word, S cross it out on their Bingo sheets. Once they have three pictures in a row, they are to shout 'Bingo'.

C. Storytelling
T narrates the story vividly. After each (double) page, T checks comprehension (»What did the monkey do on this page?«), and has S speculate about the next page (»What will the monkey do next?«). Students express their ideas.

D. Scenic acting
1. T tells S that they will act out the whole story.
2. Groups of four are formed: two actors and two teachers each.
3. The actors, who re-play the story, get a worksheet with their text (M 3). 4. After the acting, the two teachers tell the actors what they liked and give tips.

E. Relay vocabulary contest
1. Four groups are formed to consolidate the vocabulary via a relay word contest.
2. The groups are arranged in four different rows. The first student of each row tries to translate the word on the picture cards, which is raised in the air by the teacher, as fast as possible. The fastest translator of the four returns to the end of his row.
3. The game ends when every member of one group has successfully translated a picture card.

F. Homework
T: »Cut out the pictures from the worksheet and glue them into your vocabulary folder.«

3 Materials

M 1: Picture cards (selection)

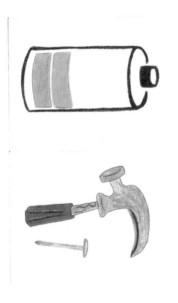

M 2: Bingo Worksheet

WiFi	to scroll	to blog
to tweet	letter	library
screen	to charge	to fix

to charge	letter	to blog
screen	WiFi	to tweet
to fix	library	to scroll

letter	to tweet	to charge
to scroll	to fix	WiFi
library	screen	to blog

library	WiFi	screen
to fix	to charge	to tweet
to blog	letter	to scroll

M 3: Text (also cf. www.lanesmithbooks.com)

Lane Smith: It's a Book
It's a mouse
It's a jackass
It's a monkey

Jackass: What do you have there?
Monkey: It's a book.

Jackass: How do you scroll down?
Monkey: I don't. I turn the page. It's a book.
Jackass: Do you blog with it?
Monkey: No, it's a book.

Jackass: Where's your mouse?
Jackass: Can you make the characters fight?
Monkey: Nope. Book.
Jackass: Can it text?
Monkey: No.
Jackass: Tweet?
Monkey: No.
Jackass: Wi-Fi?
Monkey: No.
Jackass: Can it do this? Tooooooot
Monkey: No ...
Monkey: it's a book. Look.

»Arrrrrrrrrr,« nodded Long John Silver, »we're in agreement then?« He
unsheathed his broad cutlass laughing a maniacal laugh, »Ha! Ha! Ha!«
Jim was petrified.
The end was upon him.
Then in the distance, a ship!
A wide smile played across the lad's face.

Jackass: Too many letters. I'll fix it.
                  »LJS: rrr! K? lol!
                  JIM: ☺ ! ☺«

Jackass:	So...
	What else can this book do?
	Does it need a password?
Monkey:	No.
Jackass:	Need a screen name?
Monkey:	No.
	It's a book.
Monkey:	Are you going to give my book back?
Jackass:	No.
Monkey:	Fine.
Monkey:	I'm going to the library
Jackass:	Don't worry, I'll charge it up when I'm done!
Mouse:	YOU DON'T HAVE TO...
	IT'S A BOOK, JACKASS.

Bibliography

Bader, Barbara (1976). American Picturebooks from Noah's Ark to the Beast within. New York: Macmillan.

Enever, Janet (2006). Picture Books and Young Learners of English. Münchener Arbeiten zur Fremdsprachen-Forschung 14. München: Langenscheidt.

Nespeca, Sue/Reeve, Joan (2003). Picture Books Plus: 100 Extension Activities in Art, Drama, Music, Math, and Science. Chicago: American Library Association.

Peterson, Shelley/Swartz, Larry (2008). Good Books Matter: How to Choose and Use Children's Literature to Help Students Grow as Readers. Markham: Pembroke Publishers.

Silvey, Anita (ed.) (1995). Children's Books and their Creators. Boston: Houghton Mifflin.

Smith, Lane. Bio. http://www.lanesmithooks.com/LaneSmithBooks/Bio.html. (01/08/2015)

Smith, Lane. FAQ. http://www.lanesmithbooks.com/LaneSmithBooks/FAQ.html. (01/08/2015)

Contributors

Dr. Senem Aydin

Senem Aydin graduated from Hacettepe University in Ankara, Department of English Language Teaching in 2002. She holds a M.A. and PhD degree in TEFL from the University of Munich, specializing on nonverbal communication and teacher training.

She has been teaching and pursuing a postdoctoral degree at the Chair for TEFL, Augsburg University, since 2010. Her teaching experience includes courses about individual differences, intercultural learning, research methods, and multilingualism in TEFL. Her postdoctoral project focuses on multilingual learners of English as a foreign language in a German school context.

Bernard Brown

Bernard Brown spent the first years of his career teaching English to adults in England, Italy and France before coming to Germany. He has spent most of his teaching life teaching at the 'vocationally oriented sixth form college' (his rather ungainly translation for 'Berufliche Oberschule'!) in Bad Tölz.

In addition to his fulfilling career as a teacher, in the last thirty–two years, Bernard has held hundreds of workshops for teachers in Germany, Austria and Northern Italy. He is the author or coauthor of a number of books, which have become bestsellers: *The Fun Factor; The Pleasure Principle; Begin with a smile; Pepper and Salt and Magic and More.* The titles of these books show us what Bernard's central aim is: to help teachers reduce 'the anxiety factor' and increase 'the fun factor' in the English lesson and so increase effective learning, helping even the weakest and least motivated pupils to progress in their learning.

Prof. Dr. Anita Fetzer

ANITA FETZER is a full Professor of Applied Linguistics at the University of Augsburg, Germany. She received her Ph. D. from Stuttgart University in 1993 and her habilitation in 2003, and is currently engaged in research projects on discourse connectivity and follow-ups in political discourse. Her research interests focus on pragmatics, discourse connectivity, functional grammar, and contrastive analysis.

Her most recent publications are *The Dynamics of Political Discourse* (2015, with Elda Weizman and Lawrence N. Berlin), *Political Discourse in the Media* (2007, with Gerda Lauerbach), and *Context and Appropriateness* (2007). She is editor of the book series *Pragmatics & Beyond: New Series,* associate editor of the journal *Language and Dialogue,* and a member of several editorial boards.

Prof. Dr. Petra Kirchhoff

PETRA KIRCHHOFF is Professor of Teaching English as a Foreign Language. She joined the faculty of Regensburg University in 2013. Her main research interests are the use of literature in language learning, listening comprehension in action and teacher education.

Dr. Timo Müller

TIMO MÜLLER teaches American Studies at the University of Augsburg, Germany, where he received his doctorate in 2009. His research focuses on modernism, environmental studies, and Black Atlantic literatures. He is author of *The Self as Object in Modernist Fiction: James — Joyce — Hemingway* (2010) and co-editor of *English and American Studies: Theory and Practice* (2012) and *Literature, Ecology, Ethics: Recent Trends in Ecocriticism* (2012).

Stephanie Schaidt

STEPHANIE SCHAIDT is currently research assistant and PhD student at the Chair of English Didactics, University of Augsburg. She studied English, Geography and German as a Second Language. Her research interests include teaching (children's) literature, cultural and global learning.

Katrin Stadlinger-Kessel

Born in West Berlin 1953, KATRIN STADLINGER-KESSEL grew up in New York and Munich. She chose to become a teacher for English and History and has been teaching students of different levels and age groups since then. She favours a holistic approach to teaching and employs a wide range of dynamic and creative methods in the classroom.

Prof. Dr. Carola Surkamp

CAROLA SURKAMP is Professor of TEFL (Teaching English as a Foreign Language) at the University of Goettingen, Germany. After her studies in English, French and Spanish at the Universities of Cologne and Nantes (France), she taught English Literature and Film at the University of Giessen. She is the co-author of various books on the use of literature and films in the foreign language classroom, among them *Englische Literatur unterrichten 1: Grundlagen und Methoden* (⁴2016; with Ansgar Nünning) and *Filme im Englischunterricht: Grundlagen, Methoden, Genres* (2011; with Roswitha Henseler and Stefan Möller). She also edited the encyclopedia *Metzler Lexikon Fremdsprachendidaktik* (2010). Her main research interests include literature and film in the EFL classroom and at university, teaching reading, drama activities in language learning and (inter) cultural learning.

Prof. Dr. Engelbert Thaler

ENGELBERT THALER is full Professor of TEFL at Augsburg University. After teaching English at Gymnasium for 20 years, he did his doctoral thesis on *Musikvideoclips im Englischunterricht* and his habilitation at Ludwig-Maximilians-Universität, Munich on *»Offene Lernarrangements im Englischunterricht. Rekonstruktion, Konstruktion, Konzeption, Exemplifikation, Integration«*.
His research foci are improving teaching quality *(Balanced Teaching)*, teacher education and training, developing coursebooks, media literacy, and teaching literature. He has published more than 500 contributions to TEFL. His recent publications include *Englisch unterrichten, Teaching English with Films*, and *Standard-basierter Englischunterricht*. Thaler is also editor of the journal *Praxis Fremdsprachenunterricht* and of several coursebooks.